Critical Thinking in Psychology

Research Methods and Design in Psychology

Critical Thinking in Psychology series – titles in the series

Critical Thinking in Psychology

Research Methods and Design in Psychology

**Paul Richardson, Emma Vine
and Allen Goodwin**

Series Editor: Dominic Upton

LearningMatters

First published in 2011 by Learning Matters Ltd

British Library Cataloguing in Publication Data
A CIP record for this book is available from the British Library

ISBN 978 0 85725 469 6

This book is also available in the following formats:

Adobe ebook   ISBN: 978 0 85725 471 9
ePUB ebook   ISBN: 978 0 85725 470 2
Kindle   ISBN: 978 0 85725 472 6

Cover and text design by Toucan Design
Project management by Diana Chambers
Typeset by Kelly Winter
Printed and bound in Great Britain by Shortrun Press Ltd, Exeter, Devon

Learning Matters Ltd
20 Cathedral Yard
Exeter EX1 1HB
Tel: 01392 215560
E-mail: info@learningmatters.co.uk
www.learningmatters.co.uk

FSC
www.fsc.org
MIX
Paper from
responsible sources
FSC® C014540

Contents

Acknowledgements

Paul Richardson: to H, L, J, N and J – happy reading!

Emma Vine: I would like to thank my family and colleagues for their support and patience during the writing of this book.

Allen Goodwin: to all those who have showed me patience and given me their time, especially SS and CMT. Many thanks to you all.

Grateful thanks to Emma Preece for contributing information and activities to Chapters 2 and 7.

Series editor's introduction

Studying psychology at degree level

Being a student of psychology is an exciting experience – the study of mind and behaviour is a fascinating and sprawling journey of discovery. Yet, studying psychology at degree level brings with it new experiences, skills and knowledge. This book, one in a comprehensive new series, brings you this psychological knowledge, but importantly it also brings with it directions and guidance on the skills and experiences you should also be developing during your studies.

Psychology is a growing discipline – in scope, breadth and numbers. It is one of the fastest growing subjects to study at GCSE and A level, and the number of students studying the subject at university has grown considerably over the past decade. Indeed, psychology is now one of the most popular subjects in UK higher education, with the most recent data suggesting that there are some 45,000 full-time students currently enrolled on such programmes (compiled from Higher Education Statistics Agency (HESA); statistics available at www.HESA.ac.uk) and it is likely that this number has not yet peaked.

The popularity of psychology is related to a number of reasons, not the least of which is its scope and breadth – psychology is a sprawling discipline that seeks to analyse the human mind and behaviour, which is fascinating in its own right. Furthermore, psychology aims to develop other skills – numeracy, communication and critical analysis to name but a few. For these reasons, many employers seek out psychology graduates – they bring a whole host of skills to the workplace and any activities in which they may be involved. This book brings together the knowledge base associated with psychology along with these critical skills. By reading this book, and engaging with the exercises, you will develop these skills and, in this way, will do two things: excel in your studies and your assessments, and put yourself at the front of the queue of psychology graduates when it comes to demonstrating these skills to potential employers.

Developing higher-level skills

Only about 15 to 20 per cent of psychology graduates end up working as professional psycho-logists. The subject is a useful platform for many other careers because of the skills it helps you to develop. It is useful to employers because of its subject-specific skills – knowing how people act is pertinent in almost any job and is particularly relevant to those that involve working directly with people. Psychology also develops a number of generic and transferable skills that are both essential to effective undergraduate study and valuable to employers. These include higher-level intellectual skills, such as critical and creative thinking, reflection, evaluation and analysis, and other skills such as communication, problem solving, understanding and using data, decision-making, organisational skills, teamworking and IT skills.

The Quality Assurance Agency in Higher Education (QAA) subject benchmarks for psychology (www.qaa.ac.uk/academicinfrastructure/benchmark/honours/psychology.asp), which set out the expectations of a psychology degree programme, highlight the sorts of skills with which your degree should equip you. The British Psychological Society (BPS), which accredits your degree course, acknowledges that graduate employability is an important area of focus for universities and expects that opportunities for skills development should be well embedded within your programme of study. Indeed, this is a major focus of your study – interesting as psychology is, you will need and want employment at the end of your degree.

The activities in this book have been designed to help you build the underpinning skills that you need in order to become an independent and lifelong learner, and to meet the relevant requirements of your programme of study, the QAA benchmarks and the needs of both you and your potential employer.

Many students find it a challenge to develop these skills, often learning them out of context of their study of the core knowledge domains of psychology. The activities in this book aim to help you to learn these skills at the same time as developing your core psychology knowledge, giving you opportunities continuously to practise skills so that they become second nature to you. The tasks provide guidance on what the skill is, how to develop basic competence in it and how to progress to further expertise. At the same time, development of these skills will enable you to better understand and retain the core content of your course – being able to evaluate, analyse and interpret content is the key to deepening understanding.

The skills that the activities in this book will help you to develop are as presented in Table 0.1.

In addition to review and essay questions, each chapter in this book will contain novel learning activities. Your responses will be guided through these activities and you will then be able to apply these skills within the context of developmental psychology.

Table 0.1: Skills developed in this book

Intellectual skills	Other skills
• Critical and creative thinking	• Communication: oral, visual and written
• Reflection	• Problem solving
• Analysing and evaluating	• Understanding and using data
	• Decision-making
	• Organisational skill
	• Teamwork
	• Information technology
	• Independent learning

Features in this book

At the start of each chapter there is a list of **learning outcomes**. These are a set of bullet points that highlight the outcomes you should achieve – both skills and knowledge – if you read and engage with the chapter. This will mean at the outset of the chapter that we try to orientate you, the reader, and demonstrate the relevance of the topic.

We have also included learning features throughout the individual chapters in order to demonstrate key points and promote your learning.

- **Bulleted lists** are used within the chapter to convey key content messages.

- **Case studies** are included as part of a critical thinking activity.

- **Tasks** are a series of short review questions on the topic that will help you assess yourself and your current level of knowledge – use these to see if you can move on or whether you need to reread and review the material.

- **Critical thinking activities** allow for the review of the text by encouraging key critical and creative thinking about the psychology material presented, and provide development of the generic skills. Each of these activities is followed by a **Critical thinking review** which unpicks the activity for you, showing how it should have been tackled, the main skill it develops and other skills you may have used in completing the activity.

- **Skill builder activities** use the psychology material presented in the text but focus on one particular transferable skill as outlined in Table 0.1. Each of these activities is followed by a **Skill builder review** which may provide further hints and which makes explicit the skills it helps to develop and the benefits of completing the activity.

At the end of the chapter there will also be some pedagogic features that you will find useful in developing your abilities.

- **Assignments** assess your awareness and understanding of the topic through a series of questions for you to discuss and debate with your colleagues. You can also use these questions as revision materials.

- **Summary: what you have learned** appears at the end of each chapter as a series of bullet points. We hope that these summaries will match the learning outcomes presented at the outset of the chapter.

- **Further reading** includes items that will provide additional information – some of these are in journals and some are full texts. For each we have provided the rationale for suggesting the additional reading and we hope that these will direct you accordingly.

- **Glossary** entries are highlighted in bold in the text on their first appearance.

- Finally, there is a full set of **references** to support all of the material presented in this text.

We hope you enjoy this text, which is part of a series of textbooks covering the complete knowledge base of psychology.

Professor Dominic Upton
September 2011

Introduction

Overview

This Introduction will provide a general overview of the book, and suggest ways in which you can maximise the benefits of your very astute selection! This book will facilitate your learning of the uses (and abuses) of both quantitative and qualitative research methods – a key area that underpins your psychology degree. We will discuss the various aspects involved in designing and conducting an experiment, helping you to design your own experiments and appraise those carried out by others. We will show you how this book not only enhances your knowledge of research methods, but also encourages your critical reading of published studies in any module you study.

By the end of this book you should:

- *be able to identify the types of variables used in research investigations;*
- *know how to implement the different types of experimental designs;*
- *be cognisant of ethical issues in research;*
- *be aware of the differences, similarities and benefits of using quantitative and qualitative types of research strategies;*
- *be mindful of common problems and the challenges inherent to research;*
- *have developed your organisational skills;*
- *have refined your creative and critical thinking abilities;*
- *have practised your problem-solving skills;*
- *have honed your analytical and evaluative capabilities;*
- *know how to communicate findings from a project via a written lab report.*

About the book

This book was written with the express intention of providing an accessible and critical overview of research methods. Yet too often we hear students complaining that this subject is irrelevant to psychology and their own interests – they want to learn more about dynamic topics such as how Freud's portrayal of clashes between the dark, primal and instinctive forces of the id and the restrictive, morally upright aims of the superego can forge the personality of an individual; they want to be taught the root causes of disorders such as schizophrenia and autism; brain:behaviour relationships; why people may act differently in group situations; how studying animals may possibly inform us as to our own behaviour. In contrast, the research methods modules are often considered to be dull, or they may even induce cold sweats and a rising sense of fear in some students.

However, we feel research methods is a much maligned subject, often misunderstood and not given due credit. Conducting research is how we advance our understanding and knowledge of any given area; we need to tweak and manipulate variables and measures reactions and responses to these factors in order to see how they are linked. Without new research studies being published, we cannot make any progress. Research underpins every other module you will be taught on your psychology course. Therefore learning how to conduct research, how to craft and design studies appropriately, and how to develop your ability to critique the findings and interpretations of others are all borne out of studying research methods.

In Chapter 1 we will examine the processes involved in the acquisition and definition of a research question leading to the development of the research hypothesis. Inherent problems in the operationalisation of the research will be discussed in relation to issues such as validity and reliability. At the end of this chapter, we hope that you will be aware of the reasons why there is no such thing as the perfect research design.

We then introduce the vitally important but often misunderstood topic of ethics in Chapter 2. Ethics often seems to be a rather lofty and philosophical area, but an understanding of ethics will help you gain a better understanding of why some psychology studies are carried out, why some are not, and why we cannot always do the things that early psychological researchers were able to do. An in-depth understanding of ethics is important, not just for your own research, but also to have a better understanding of all the research that you read throughout your studies. It is too easy to think of ethics as something that someone else makes decisions about. Instead, if you can think of ethics as a dynamic process of which you can be a part, it will help you to evaluate the ethics of research you read, and also to consider the ethics of your own studies better.

Moving on from considering the ethical issues inherent in research, we begin to tackle some of the more basic concepts you need to learn. In Chapter 3 we introduce 'variables' – the cornerstone of research studies. We define exactly what they are, how they can be used in research, how we can manipulate and alter them and how we can measure them. You will learn how there are different types of variables (including the ones best avoided), and how, despite our best efforts, there will always be a degree of error in our measurements.

Once you are knowledgeable about variables, we then incorporate this knowledge into learning how to design an experiment in Chapter 4. Experiments can be used to demonstrate cause and effect – how changing one variable may affect another. You will see how this simple premise has profound implications for advancing our knowledge. There are a variety of different experimental designs that can be utilised in research studies. You may well already be aware that some designs have groups of different people (participants), while others rely on the same group but are tested on multiple occasions. It is even possible to combine these two approaches. We outline how each design has a particular set of advantages and disadvantages. We discuss these aspects in order to facilitate you when designing your own experiments and help you to critically appraise experimental research studies carried out by others. An offshoot of these experimental designs is found in the study of developmental psychology. In Chapter 5 we examine these time course studies and learn that a central theme of this area is to measure age-related changes and plot the developmental trajectories of abilities and skills across the lifespan. If we strip away the change in terminology, it is possible to reveal that these designs are merely variations on those already learned in the previous chapter.

You may often come across situations in which, due to a variety of ethical, technological, financial or pragmatic reasons, it is not possible to conduct a cause-and-effect experiment. In Chapter 6 we discuss how it is possible to sidestep these issues and assess the relationships or the degree of association between two or more variables with a different approach – one that can also be used to predict future scores based on current results.

We then switch tack from using designs that rely on measuring quantifiable changes in behaviour and performance to designs that are qualitative. In Chapter 7 we introduce the basics of qualitative design. This chapter will help you to understand what qualitative methods are, why we use them, and the strengths and weaknesses of the qualitative approach. If you understand why we use qualitative methods, you will have a grounding to build on when you read about qualitative data collection and analysis. Later in this book, you will also learn about mixed methods design, and an understanding of qualitative methods will help in your appreciation of this growing area.

We then progress from this introduction to qualitative designs in order to present some of the types of qualitative data that exist, and how it is possible to collect them. Chapter 8 introduces some of the main data collection methods in qualitative methods. You will be able to see that the different data gathering methods can provide very different and very rich data sets.

Having acquired qualitative data, the next logical step in this sequence is becoming familiar with how to analyse it. In Chapter 9 you will start to understand how to go about analysing the data that you have collected. The last three chapters of the book show you that the qualitative approaches take an integrated view of research questions, data collection and analysis. You will also see that the qualitative approach, while it is not conventionally 'scientific' in the same way as experiments are, is nonetheless systematic in its execution.

Chapters 4 to 9 present a variety of quantitative and qualitative designs as though they are separate entities. However, in Chapter 10 we will examine how it is possible to combine these differing approaches in order to extend our learning of a given topic under investigation. Despite their apparent philosophical differences, we will consider how these mixed method approaches can complement each other. We examine the basis behind the assumption of mixed methods being the preferential methodological approach, and question whether this is true of all research topics.

In Chapter 11, we explore some of the common problems associated with research. We discuss the problems of missing data along with the possible solutions to this. We examine the importance of the identification of outliers, along with parametric assumptions. Finally, in the context of type I and type II errors we highlight the issue that findings of statistical non-significance may not be indicative of poor design but lack of statistical power and the importance of clearly identifying the difference between statistical reality and psychological reality.

The final chapter of this book deals with the final stage of any research study: writing it up. In Chapter 12 we consider why writing a research report is an absolute necessity – how it is a vehicle to communicate your findings to a wider audience. We examine the different sections that are typically found in a research report, and illustrate what information needs to given in these. We also consider the areas of weakness and mistakes that students often make so that you are best placed to avoid repeating them.

We hope you enjoy this book as much as we have enjoyed writing it!

Paul Richardson, Emma Vine and Allen Goodwin

Chapter 1

Designing psychological research studies

Learning outcomes

This chapter will outline the phases and problems associated with the early stage of conducting research. It will take you through the process of finding, defining and designing a research question and highlight the factors that need to be considered.

By the end of this chapter you should:

- *understand the stages involved in setting up a research study;*
- *be able to undertake the process of finding, defining and designing a research study;*
- *understand the importance of a literature review in the process of conducting research;*
- *understand the need for a formal operationalisation of the research question;*
- *be aware of the problems of capturing a measure;*
- *be aware of the issues of validity, reliability and confounds.*

Introduction

The statement that 'Good researchers are made, not born' is worth keeping in mind when you approach the design of research studies. Far too often it is assumed that the ability to conduct research is somehow innate or easy. The truth is far more brutal – good research is a process based on acquired knowledge and experience. In order to make this whole process less daunting, we can start by fragmenting the research process into discrete steps. The reasons are twofold. The first is that to approach the process as a whole entity may be beyond our cognitive ability (there are only a limited number of cognitive balls that we can juggle). Secondly, through the categorisation of each stage, we can minimise errors that we may make along the way. It is important to realise that the use of the most sophisticated statistical analysis does not compensate for a badly framed **research question** or poor methodology, as these invalidate any statistical finding. Always remember that the statistical analysis conducted on the data obtained is only as good as the quality of the data. If the gathered data is flawed, then the findings will also be.

Taking this into account, let us consider the research process as a set of stages outlined below.

- Finding a research question.

- The inevitable literature review.

- Generation of the hypothesis.

- Sampling.

- The operationalisation of the research question.

- **Validity**, **reliability** and confounds.

Finding a research question

Without a clearly defined research question, there is no research. The struggle is how to even get to that point. This is where two important aspects of the researcher (you) come in: interest and knowledge.

A good starting point is the reason for the researcher's areas of interest. It may be that you observed a social situation where something unexpected occurred. What caused that particular outcome? What were the dynamics involved? Alternatively, while reading some recently published research, a question may present itself – something that you read did not make sense. Finally, abandoning personal interest, it could be that you were hired to conduct a piece of research on a predefined question. The sources of inspiration for a research question can be potentially boundless, limited only by the extent to which you wear your 'researcher's hat' when interacting with the world around you. The second aspect – 'knowledge' – is the part that requires con-siderable effort and hard work. The last thing that you want to do is ask a question that has already been answered, and the only way you can be certain of this is to have an up-to-date knowledge of the area. Conducting a literature review is the most effective way of attaining this. In addition, it will also help in writing up the traditional undergraduate laboratory or research report.

The literature review

If the area of interest is new to you, then it may be of use initially to use an undergraduate psychology textbook that deals with the global aspects and themes of the area of interest. This will allow you to get a good feel for the general areas of contention. Importantly within the text, specific references will be made to primary sources of research (the original research written up by the researchers themselves) directly related in a more focused way to your 'research question to be'. However, there will be a time when you have to enter the world of the online refereed journal.

Academic institutions spend a great deal of money on online peer-reviewed journals, which can be accessed from a variety of online databases (for example, Psychlit, PsychINFO, Science Direct etc.). Interrogation of these online databases is an essential stage yet is also a time-consuming process, which requires identifying the relevant material from that which is irrelevant. However, there are a few tricks that more experienced researchers employ in order to facilitate the gathering of relevant information.

The first is to search for review journal articles. These are journal articles in which experts in a particular field have already reviewed the relevant material, examined the contradictions inherent to any area, and come up with an overall considered, educated and well-argued conclusion. There are two main types of review article – the classic literature review article and the meta-analysis (for a discussion of the advantages of the meta-analytic review, see Rosenthal (1991)). What both have in common is a considerable list of related articles within the .reference section that can be plundered to gain more knowledge of the area.

The second trick is the use of keywords. Once you have found a relevant article related to your research interest, you will find, often at the bottom of the abstract, a list of words. These are keywords, which are tags or descriptors related to the article. Related articles will have the same tags or keywords. These can then be used in order to search online databases. The third trick is the use of the citation index. If an article you have identified as relevant to your area of research has been cited by other proceeding articles, then there is a good chance that these later works will also contain material relevant to your area of interest.

Using these three main methods of gathering material, you should be able to gather a considerable amount of relevant material and identify numerous ideas for research. It is also possible that your original research idea may have been answered or that a more interesting question has come to light. Now comes the next step of forming a clearly defined research hypothesis.

The research hypothesis

So what is the research hypothesis? In the simplest terms, a hypothesis is a statement of the predicted outcome of a **manipulation**. Of course, the manipulation can be an inherent characteristic of the participant (for example, gender, football team supporter or music preference) or an active manipulation (for example, drug dosage, stress manipulation). A hypothesis makes the assumption that there is a specific relationship between the manipulation of the **experimental conditions** and the observed (or measured) outcome. Formally, there are always two types of hypothesis – the **null hypothesis** (H_o) and the **experimental hypothesis** (H_e) (or **alternative hypothesis** (H_a)). There is always at least one experimental hypothesis for each type of manipulation, otherwise more formally known as the **independent variable** or factor (see Chapter 4 for further explanation). The null hypothesis, although usually more formally stated, expresses that the manipulation has no effect upon the measured outcome (referred to as the **dependent variable**). An important thing to note is that we never test an experimental hypothesis but rather reject or fail to reject the null hypothesis. This may seem rather odd until you realise that with the statistical tests that we employ as research methodologists, we are testing the extent to which the outcome of a manipulation (experimental condition) could have happened due to chance. It is only when this is so unlikely as to happen by chance that we refute the null hypothesis and 'accept' the experimental hypothesis as the only other credible alternative.

Now, consider the following example. Researchers are interested in courage and (after a great deal of research) were convinced that there was a difference in innate courage between 'contact' and 'non-contact' sport players. They wanted to test this empirically. In order to state this research idea formally, they generated the following hypotheses:

> Null hypothesis: (H_o): There will be no difference in the innate courage between 'contact' and 'non-contact' sport players.

> Experimental hypothesis (H_e): There will be a difference in innate courage between 'contact' and 'non-contact' sport players.

In the above experimental hypothesis, there is no attempt to state any direction of outcome in relation to how type of sport played reflects innate courage. We refer to this as a two-tailed hypothesis. This is because we do not **infer** the direction of causality. This is where we could argue that, as true scientists, we keep an open mind to the possibility that the results may be unexpected. There is also a statistical implication of not having a two-tailed hypothesis – in short, it is easier to demonstrate statistical significance if the hypothesis is directional, something that we as researchers need to take into account when reading other research. A directional hypothesis (or unidirectional hypothesis) is one where the direction of the effect is clearly stated. We might therefore write the above hypothesis as:

> H_e: Those with a high level of innate courage will play 'contact' sports when compared to those who play 'non-contact' sports.

Here we can clearly see that we are predicting the exact nature of the outcome of our research. So let us stick to our non-directional, or two-tailed, hypothesis. The next step in our research is to work out how we will measure heroism and courage, and all the pitfalls and fun that might entail. We now need to **operationalise** our research question with formal **operational definitions**. But first, let us consider where our participants may come from.

Samples, sampling and populations

With any piece of research, it is impossible to ask everyone in the world to take part to ensure that our results apply to everyone. Therefore, we do the next best thing – we take a sample of individuals from a specified **population**. The use of 'population' as a term may seem odd; what we mean by population is what represents its defining characteristic. For example, the population of psychology students refers to all those individuals (with all their other individual differences) who study psychology. We could also have a sample of a population of left-handed individuals, males, females, psychology students or, even more specifically, female, left-handed psychology students. How and what we define as being the population is dependent on our research question and reflects the characteristics of interest of our pool of individuals from whom we will sample. How we sample, and the number of participants that we recruit, may have implications for the validity and reliability of our research. It is important to make sure that our sampling is unbiased and representative (that all the differences in ability/scores/attitudes due to individual differences are as widely distributed as that of the population from which we have sampled).

The preferred method of sampling is called **random sampling**. Random sampling is when all individuals within a population have the same chance of being included in the research as a participant. With a sufficient sample size, a random sample has the most likelihood of reflecting the range of data as found in the population as a whole. Although this method is preferable to other methods of sampling, it is often the most expensive and not possible due to financial constraints. A common mistake is to confuse random sampling with **random allocation**. Random allocation is where the participants are allocated to one or more conditions randomly in order to minimise the effect that individual differences may have upon the research outcome.

It is more likely that some sort of **quota convenience sampling** or **opportunistic sampling** will be used. This is where participants are recruited as conveniently as possible (for example, through poster advertisements, direct contact or the internet etc.) and a specified number has been set by the researcher. Although problems may arise with this method, it is one of the most practical and efficient methods of quickly recruiting participants. However, with this method greater care must be taken to avoid unrepresentative placement of participants across the different conditions. It may even be worth considering exclusion criteria. For example, should psychology students be allowed to take part in psychology-based research? Does their possible knowledge of certain areas automatically preclude them from taking part? Whatever the sampling method, we infer that the results and findings obtained from our recruited **cohort** apply to the population as a whole. Therefore, if there is an inherent flaw in our recruitment of participants, then our results cannot be inferred on methodological grounds to be generalisable to the population as a whole.

Task —| Researchers wished to test the effect of a new learning strategy on high-speed learning. In order to test the effectiveness of this new technique, they recruited 70 participants. They then allocated 35 participants to each of the two following conditions: a **control condition** whereby the participants were not trained in this new technique, and a trained condition where they would receive training.

When they analysed the data, they found no difference in technique on performance. They did not realise that in the control condition, 27 of the 35 participants belonged to a memory masters club that specialised in memory training.

> ├ Why may there have been no difference in performance found? How might this result from bad design have been avoided if the same participants had taken part?
>
> ├ How would you design this research to avoid this error in the future?

Operationalisation of the research question

The operationalisation of the research question reflects the 'nuts and bolts' aspect of research. This is where there is an explicit statement of the participant population (for example, conducted on psychology students), how sampled, the experimental procedure undertaken and, very importantly, which measures were used. The importance of stating exactly how and which measures are used are important aspects of psychological research. Two main problems confront us.

1. All measurement contains error.

2. Which measures do we use?

All measurement contains error

The first point is the simple realisation that in any measurement we have two sources of potential error: systematic and random (also see Chapter 3). For example, when measuring the height of an individual, we may be using a faulty tape measure that always gives a reading 20 per cent less than it should be. In this case, all the measurements made will be systematically less than is the case in reality (**systematic error**) as some factor is acting on our results in a systematic manner that we may not be aware of. Alternatively, the researcher may not be paying attention (they may be uncharacteristically nervous around the person that they are measuring) and therefore may not record the height correctly. In this case, there is **random error**. This is, by default, unsystematic and can make the results obtained unreliable. In most research, we consider that random error can be minimised through increasing our number of measurements (participants).

Which measures do we use?

Whenever we measure something in psychological research, we make an assumption (hopefully based upon good theoretical assumptions) that our measurement taps into the question that we are asking. In some instances, a single simple measure may be used: blood pressure as an indication of stress level, or galvanic skin response as an indication of arousal. However, often psychologists are required to measure more tricky aspects of human performance or behaviour. We have to measure a **construct**. Let us examine this by returning to the study mentioned above, in which we are interested in the level of courage and the frequency of heroic behaviour. The first question to be asked is, 'What defines courage?', followed quickly by a second interwoven question, 'How do we measure our definition?' Although we can buy 'Courage' in pints, we are not interested in that form of courage, so that is not the definition that we are interested in. We have to be clear about what we mean by the term courage, for example, 'Courage is the ability to confront fear'. This becomes our working definition.

We now need to consider how to measure courage. As we cannot directly measure courage through physical means, much like other psychological concepts such as introversion, extroversion and quality of life, we have to decide how best to measure it. It is highly unlikely that a complex psychological dimension can be captured by the use of a single measure (a single question or observation). It is more likely that we would use multiple measures, each of which independently would not be perfect in capturing courage, but which, when combined, would, we hope, accurately capture those aspects that signify a courageous individual. We would need a whole battery of questions rather than a single one. Which measures we use are always informed by past research and contain a strong underpinning of theory. Once these measures, whatever form they take, have been decided, we state them clearly to form an operational definition (Judd et al., 1991) of courage. This operational definition sets out how our working definition is constructed; how our construct of courage is measured.

Task — Constructs, theoretical assumptions and measurement

Patient: I am ill, doctor!

Doctor: Let's just put this thermometer in to find out, shall we?

- To what extent does measurement of temperature indicate good health?

- What does the thermometer actually measure?

- What are the possible sources of systematic error?

- What are the possible sources of unsystematic error?

- How is good health inferred?

Task — Researchers wished to investigate the development of memory capacity throughout the first ten years of life. Children of particular age groups, 2–4, 5–7 and 8–10, were selected. A simple memory test was presented where the children had to learn a list of items (the researchers read out the list in each case) and recall them a few minutes later.

- What may be the problem in presenting the same test to all age groups?
- What are the possible sources of systematic error?
- What are the possible sources of unsystematic error?

Issues of validity, reliability and confounding variables

Having decided which measures to use in your research, other important considerations come into play. These are issues of validity, reliability and the possible influence of confounds (see Chapter 6 and Chapter 3 respectively). Validity is the expression of the extent to which you can be sure that you are measuring what is intended. Reliability relates to how durable and consistent the measures are over time. Finally, confounds are the researcher's nightmare, and are those factors that we unintentionally measure which may influence our results to such an extent that our findings are void. We shall deal with each of these in turn.

Validity

Construct validity

Let us return to our experiment above in which we are interested in the measurement of courage. How do we maximise our construct validity? We may have a set of questions that we have asked as well as a set of directly observable measures (for example, heart rate in response to noxious stimuli). However, each measure will not just measure 'pure' courage, but will most likely measure additional factors. The only way in which we can hope to capture courage is to use a multitude of measures so that all of what we define courage to be is captured. In this attempt to capture the construct of courage, we will inadvertently also capture some unrelated factors, which have nothing to do with our construct of interest. High construct validity will exhibit convergence in that the pattern of scores will be similar (convergent) for all those measures that are theoretically presumed to measure the construct of interest (courage). This, of course, can be tested through examining to what extent the scores are correlated. If the pattern of responses is dissimilar or divergent, we may have to consider that the measures that we used may not be capturing our intended measure. In addition, if we found that our measure of courage was strongly correlated with measures of intelligence, then the question arises as to whether the measure of courage was merely a measure of intelligence. In this instance, we would not want similar patterns of responses.

In order to maximise construct validity, more than one measure should be taken whenever possible. Of course, it may not always be appropriate but you should always be critical in the evaluation of the measure used. The use of multiple measures (especially in relation to complex personality traits) with different scales (for example, Thurstone, 1929; Guttman, 1944; Likert, 1932) or the Semantic Differential Scale (Osgood et al., 1957) allows for a thorough examination of the validity of the construct to be undertaken in relation to the pattern of responses given across all observers. The pattern of responses given should always be theoretically justified.

Task — To what extent does an examination measure our construct of 'knowledge of a certain area'? What other factor may examinations be testing?

Internal validity

This relates to what extent causality can be inferred. To what extent can heroism be determined by courage? Formally, we are asking if a change in A leads to a change in B. If we are sure that this is the case, then we have high **internal validity**. As researchers, we have to ask the critical question, 'Is there an equally plausible alternative explanation?' For example, if we found that the relationship between sport preference (contact or non-contact) and courage was mediated by a factor such as intelligence, we cannot be sure of the direct relationship. We therefore have low internal validity. Threats to internal validity come from a variety of sources such as selection, maturation, mortality, instrumentation, history and selection by maturation, and **confounding variables**. Let us examine these each in turn.

Selection is where the difference obtained between the conditions was not due to differences in the conditions but due to differences in the innate characteristics of the participants within each group. For example, if one of the groups had been recruited from the armed forces and the other group from the general population, the difference in courage may not have been due to the type of sport played. Arguably, it may be that those within the armed forces may have had an elevated innate level of courage (personality and/or experience), which would have affected the results.

Maturation impacts more on longitudinal studies (where people are tracked over long periods of time). It may be merely a consequence of age that certain attitudes and abilities change relative to the general population.

Instrumentation is where the measurement employed may affect the results obtained. In the case of courage, a better measure of courage may have been found and therefore used instead. The subsequent change in measure will change the results obtained. This can also apply to electronic equipment as well, and in some instances laboratory equipment needs to be calibrated at regular intervals to ensure accuracy of reading.

History is where an event outside the research question may influence or lead to a change in participant behaviour. An obvious example would be the change in attitude towards some ethnic groups before and after the 9/11 suicide attacks. Therefore, the responses that participants may give on a tolerance questionnaire may change pre and post event. Although this is a 'global' event, care should be taken to be aware that more 'local' events could affect the results of the study; even a change of research assistant can be significant if the participants no longer feel at ease with the assistant.

Selection by maturation is where there may be changes in individuals within groups over time. For example, children's differences in performance in a task may be due purely to developmental changes, a consequence of time. This is especially evident in young children as their development speeds vary considerably across relatively short spaces of time.

Confounding variables: Inherent in any research is the identification of those aspects or factors that have the greatest influence upon an outcome. However, there are times when other aspects unknown to the researcher can influence the result. For example, if different relaxation techniques were to be tested individually by different researchers, unexpected findings could ensue if the measurement of effectiveness was heart rate. One obvious factor may be the influence of the level of attractiveness and gender of the researcher upon the participant. It has not been unknown that a particular group of participants in the relaxation group had very high heart rates when compared to the high-stress group due to factors not relevant to the investigation. Often, such confounds can be negated by good methodological design – ensuring that different conditions were researcher dependent. However, researchers can never be sure that some other factor, however seemingly irrelevant, may not in some way influence the results.

Although these threats to internal validity by no means constitute an exhaustive list, they clearly indicate that good research entails careful and constant evaluation. No matter how good (or even impressive) the statistical analysis of data is, if the assumptions underpinning the data are incorrect, then the outcome of analysis will be, too. However, many of these threats to internal validity can be overcome by careful sampling and random allocation of a sufficient number of participants to each of the individual conditions. However, there may be times when you have to match participants carefully between different conditions/groups, especially when comparing the effect of an active manipulation between the experimental conditions (for example, the effect of different teaching methods) or through the use of a control condition.

Face validity

This is a subjective evaluation of how the measure appears to the participant (Judd et al., 1991) and can influence how the participant engages with the measures used. There are instances when the measure should appear to measure exactly what it does. For example, if you give children a set of puzzles and games on pieces of paper, they may engage as though it is a game (and not take it seriously) when, in fact, it is an aptitude test. In this instance, you would wish that the participants were fully aware of what you are measuring. However, there are times when you wish to hide the **face validity** in order to prevent socially desirable responses (Rosenberg, 1965). Once again, the important aspect is that it must make methodological sense whether to have high, low or non-existent face validity.

Predictive validity

A study with good **predictive validity** of its measures should predict the outcome of the measures used. For example, if there is a measure of high extroversion but, in reality, the person behaves as an introvert, then our measure of extroversion lacks in predictive validity.

External validity

This relates to what extent the finding of the research study can be applied to the population as a whole and, in addition, to other environments outside the research setting. When examining whether the findings obtained can be inferred to the population as a whole, we need to take into account the composition of our sampled participants. If we have recruited participants on some specific criteria that directly relates to the research question, then we may not be able to generalise the findings obtained to the whole population. If we recruited occipital-lobe-damaged patients and examined the way they perceived the world, we would have to be extremely cautious to infer that non-occipital-lobe-damaged patients perceived the world in the same way. In this case, the characteristics of the participants (or sample) dictate to what extent we can externalise these results to the world as a whole. This is why sampling without **bias** (see above) is important. There are individual differences within participants and we hope that with sufficient participants these biases will cancel each other out so that there is no over-riding bias that may interfere with the results. Similarly, the mere fact that psychology students are often recruited does not mean that the results cannot be extended to the population as a whole (unless, of course, you think that there is something unique to psychology students that sets them apart from the rest of humanity).

Another consideration is the environment in which the study took part. In many instances laboratories are used, quite sensibly, in order to allow for maximum control that would not be possible in a more naturalistic study (for example, the minimisation of distractions). This does not mean that these studies are automatically ecologically invalid. It all depends upon the research you are conducting. Of course, if the research was examining individual behaviour within a crowd, then it is unlikely that the strict laboratory setting would be suitable. A more naturalistic setting, through observation, might be preferable.

Two additional threats to **external validity** are **experimenter expectancy** and **demand characteristics**. A series of studies by Rosenthal (1966) and Rosenthal and Rosnow (1969) demonstrate that the researcher may have an effect upon the results obtained. This can be unconscious on the part of the researcher and reflect subtle cues that the researcher gives to the participant. Related to this are demand characteristics in which the participant aims to give the response that is most socially desirable, specific to the researcher, research question or societal norms as a whole. It is also worthwhile considering that demand characteristics and experimenter expectancy could also cross into questionnaire-based studies.

The importance of replication as an extension of external validity

Replication is often a neglected consideration in research. Its importance extends beyond validation or external validity. Since no study can be perfectly replicated (for example, variations in the participant sample), where replication does result in similar findings, this enhances the external validity of the findings. Just as importantly, findings that contradict the initial study upon replication can define the limits of its external validity. This, in turn, leads to a greater understanding of the research area.

Reliability

Test-retest reliability

As mentioned above, all measurement, whether through a questionnaire or direct measurement (for example, heart beat), contains error, which can be both systematic and random. The extent to which a single measure or multiple measures are free from random error is referred to as reliability. In order to gauge the extent of reliability from our measure, you could theoretically test the same individuals across two different time periods and examine how closely the results matched. This is referred to as **test-retest reliability**. It would be expected that a reliable test or measure would yield the same results across differing time periods. The extent of this reliability is easily quantified through correlating the scores obtained. If the reliability of the measure is perfect (without any error), then the scores would be perfectly correlated (Pearson's $r = 1$.), but this is highly unlikely. However, Kline (2000) argues that for good test-retest reliability, there should be a high level of correlation ($r > .8$) with a test-retest separation of at least three months and the involvement of a minimum of 100 participants. This approach may be problematic purely for practical reasons as participants may not be available after such a long period of time and keeping track of them may be beyond the resources of the researcher. Of course, what must also be kept into account is the effect of other factors, such as maturation or historical events (see page 69), which may further complicate matters and render a test-retest reliability measure infeasible.

Internal consistency reliability

An alternative approach when you have multiple measures of the same construct is to use what is called internal consistency reliability. This measure of reliability is typically employed when a questionnaire is used. The assumption underpinning this form of reliability is that error not only occurs across time but also across the different questions (or measures). If the source of random error is small, then the overall pattern between the responses or different questions should be small. If, however, the error is large, then there should be no systematic responses between the separate measures (a case of not hearing the conversation because of the noise). This has led to **split-half reliability** as a measure of internal consistency reliability. The problem now arises as how to split the measures. In the case of a questionnaire, for example, how do we split the questions? Do we compare the responses to the odd-numbered questions with the even-numbered questions? Alternatively, do we split the measures in half and compare the first half with the second half? The resultant reliability could therefore be influenced by how we split the measures. A solution to this is the use of **Cronbach's alpha**, which is a measure of internal consistency reliability based upon all the possible comparisons of split-half reliability. Although Kline (2000) posits that this should be close to 0.9, Clark-Carter (2010) makes arguably a more compelling justification that this should be around 0.7 but not lower.

The 'myth' of the perfect research design

Returning to our initial statement 'Good researchers are made, not born', it should be obvious that conducting good research is not a simplistic process and that many factors need to be taken into account. Many of the potential minefields and errors that could undermine your findings are usually avoided by having an in-depth understanding of the area you are researching. Remember that there is no 'perfect research design'. One thing to keep in mind while designing a research study is to ask as simple a question as possible. This does not mean simplistic research. It is better to answer a simple question well than a complex question badly. Whatever the research question, it is important that the parameters, methodology and operationalisation of the research question are clearly expressed so that it is clear exactly what was done so that others may evaluate the strength of your argument, which is the fundamental basis of what researchers call peer review.

Critical thinking activity

The reliability of sources of information

Critical thinking focus: critical and creative thinking

Key question: *What is the difference between sources of information on the internet and online refereed journals?*

With the increased availability of information on the internet, it is often tempting to utilise this rich source of potential information that is apparently available. The basic assumptions that we make in the initial stages based upon empirical (demonstrable evidence) can anchor our research question or set the focus of direction for our research. If the fundamental premise of our research question is erroneous, then the very question we ask – the research we conduct – may be flawed. Therefore, it is important to evaluate to what extent information gained from the internet is accurate.

Consider the following questions to aid your critical appraisal.

If the internet is truly reliable, why do universities purchase expensive online access to peer review journal databases?

What is the difference between an online peer-reviewed article and a non-peer-reviewed document? How can you tell the difference?

Some academic researchers have their own web pages on a university website where they have posted links (or pdf files) with currently published (or about to be published) journal articles. Are these trustworthy sources of information?

Critical thinking review

This activity helps you to develop your skills of critical and creative thinking in the process of gathering information required for a literature review. Rather than accepting information without thought, it focuses on the reliability of the information gathered. It is important to distinguish between trustworthy and untrustworthy sources of information and be able to evaluate the information as such. This exercise should help you to be able to do so, not just now but in the future.

Skill builder activity

The file drawer problem (Rosenthal, 1991)

Transferable skill focus: independent learning

Key question: *What are the implications of the file drawer problem and how might this affect our current state of knowledge?*

There is an inherent problem in relation to published peer review research that has been termed the file drawer problem. Implicit in most published research is that the findings are statistically significant. What happens when a study is conducted that finds non-significant results? More often than not, it ends up at the bottom of the filing cabinet (or placed in some obscure file on the computer hard drive) never to see the light of day.

Consider the following questions to aid your critical appraisal.

- In developing knowledge of a specific area, is it only of use to know what affects an outcome?

- If non-significance is found, is it of any use to replicate the study?

- If a published article found a statistically significant result (a rejection of the null hypothesis) and no one was able to replicate the result, what might this tell us about the initial study? How would researchers communicate this fact?

Skill builder review

This activity helps you to develop critical skills in the examination of published material. Even though the study may show a significant impact upon an outcome, you should not exclude your critical faculties in evaluating the evidence on methodological grounds or through a thorough knowledge of an area. (We will revisit this again in Chapter 11: Common problems.)

Assignments

1. All sciences should be critical in the manner in which they measure observations. To what extent may this be especially true for psychology?

This chapter highlighted the importance of a clear operationalisation of the research question and the problem of measuring behaviour. How can we be confident that what we think we measure is, in fact, what we are measuring? Should other more traditional sciences (for example, physics, chemistry) be just as critical? If not, why not?

2. To what extent is an in-depth knowledge of the area of interest vital for finding a research question?

A working knowledge of the material related to the area of interest will help in the 'finding of a research question'. However, is this sufficient? What may a good understanding of research methodology contribute, too?

3. Assuming that no single study is perfect, why do multiple studies in an area of research contribute to the overall knowledge and findings of individual studies?

Summary: what you have learned

You should now be confident that the generation of a credible research question is, to a large extent, a process that can be followed. This entails an appreciation of conducting a relevant literature review in order to shape and clearly define a research question. You should have an awareness of how sampling could potentially invalidate your findings and therefore how sampling problems can be minimised (or better, avoided altogether).

It should also be apparent that a clear operationalisation of the research question is vital, not only to minimise one's own potential for error, but to allow those who evaluate your work to be able to do so (and hopefully agree with the decisions that you have made). Alongside this is the realisation that the measures used within the research design may not be perfect; that often more than one measure will be needed to capture more complex aspects.

Finally, issues of validity (the extent to which you can be sure that you are measuring what was intended), reliability (how durable and consistent your measures are over time) and possible confounding variables were examined.

It is hoped that you will appreciate that research is an acquired rather than inherent skill, and that knowledge is acquired through the process of one small step at a time. The devil is always in the detail.

Further reading

Clark-Carter, D (2010) *Quantitative Psychological Research: The Complete Student's Handbook*, Chapter 6: Asking Questions II: Measuring Attitude and Meaning. 3rd edition. Hove: Psychology Press.

This chapter gives a clear account of the different approaches to measurement.

Chapter 2

Ethics

Learning outcomes

The purpose of this chapter is to introduce you to the principles of ethical conduct in research and to help you understand why some psychology studies are carried out, why some are not, and why we cannot always do the things that earlier researchers were able to do. An in-depth understanding of ethics is important; not only for conducting your own research, but also so that you can appreciate and critically evaluate the research that you will encounter throughout your studies. We recommend that you use this text as a point of reference when planning, conducting and reporting research.

By the end of this chapter you should:

- *understand the code of ethics as it currently applies to psychologists;*
- *gain a critical understanding of the function of the ethical code;*
- *be able to consider the problem of 'grey areas' in ethics and ethical decision-making;*
- *appreciate the problems of using data that may have been gathered unethically;*
- *have developed your problem-solving and decision-making skills;*
- *have reflected on the contribution ethics makes to research.*

Introduction

The principle objective of research is to add to an existing body of knowledge. In other words, researchers aim to increase what we know about a particular topic or contribute towards the empirical study of phenomena. Research is fundamentally important to all academic fields, including psychology. The range of things that we can investigate is boundless and is limited only by our imaginations. However, although we may be interested in all manner of things, there are limits as to what we can do, and how we can do it. All psychologists in the United Kingdom – be they student, academic or practitioner – are guided and bound by the British Psychological Society (BPS) code of ethics. Your first notable experience of these restrictions is likely to occur during the preparation and submission of your dissertation proposal. Before the ethics committee at your institution will accept the proposal, you will need to demonstrate that you have considered and implemented ethical practices. You will also need to demonstrate that the research will not bring yourself or the department into disrepute.

Hopefully, by the end of this chapter, you will have a better understanding of ethics and its role in psychology research and practice. There are two big aspects you need to understand in ethics if you are going to gain a clear and critical insight into the field. Obviously, you need to understand the BPS code of ethics as it currently stands, but you also need to understand the history of ethics. If you understand how ethics used to work (or not work!), you will better understand how it works now.

At its simplest, we could tell you to read the BPS guidelines (British Psychological Society, August 2009). However, the guidelines are dynamic; they change and adapt as our research and the world around us changes. For example, there were no social networking sites such as Facebook or Twitter 15 years ago. Today, there are numerous sites like this, although their popularity varies considerably. In fact, by the time you read this book many of these sites may have been superseded by others. The point is that the code of ethics must adapt to take changing modes of social interaction and avenues for research into account. In other words, as technology develops, and as society changes, the code of ethics has to adapt to facilitate the ethical study of these phenomena.

Another important factor that can influence the code of ethics is how our own culture changes and evolves. Our culture is dynamic; our beliefs, attitudes and norms change along with it. For example, if you look at the studies investigating homosexuality that were carried out 50 years ago, they were founded on the assumption that homosexuality was 'abnormal' and studies attempted to find reasons why people may be homosexual. Today, you will find that most of the theories and research surrounding the topic of homosexuality looks at the experiences of participants and their sexuality is treated as just another factor, rather than as an abnormality.

The BPS code of ethics can be summarised as 'treat others how you would like to be treated'. It sets out what we should and should not do, how we should treat our participants (and for practitioners, how to treat clients) and how we should conduct ourselves. How does this code affect you as a student?

Imagine that you are writing your dissertation proposal. You have decided what you want to do for your study; you have designed it, and now you have submitted your proposal for scrutiny by the ethics committee. Although the code of ethics was established by the BPS, there are various bodies that are involved in ethics at a local level. Your university will have an ethics committee and there is likely to be another ethics committee that oversees student ethics. Work that includes outside agencies (such as the NHS) will also involve an ethics committee, and should you go into postgraduate study, research-funding bodies will also have their own ethics committee. Your proposal may pass through various ethics committees and, perhaps surprisingly, they may come to different decisions. Every ethics panel or committee is made up of a number of people, usually four or more. All of these people will be well versed in ethics and the practice of research, although it is often a subjective decision process. One committee member may feel that your proposal is fine; another may have serious reservations. The committee meets to discuss these cases, and to try to find an agreement. When the committee decides that something is ethically sound, it passes it. If it has reservations, it may request changes to be made, or it may reject your proposal out of hand and you will have to rethink your application.

If the ethics panel makes the decision, why do I need to worry?

You may well be thinking 'OK, if the ethics panel is making the final decision, what does it matter if I do not get to the bottom of ethics? It will tell me where I am going wrong, and then I can rewrite from there'. However, if you view ethical decisions as someone else's responsibility, you are likely to find that research is much more difficult and the approval process is significantly longer than if you were to share the responsibility for these decisions. Ethics is a curious aspect of research. It is a subjective and philosophical area with very few absolutes, meaning that sometimes your ability to argue and support your proposal can make the difference between acceptance and rejection. The ethics decision process is a fine balance between any potential risks to the participant and the potential benefits of the research. While you are an undergraduate, the potential benefits of your research are likely to be limited. It is unlikely that your research will be published in a peer-reviewed journal or that it will make a major impact upon the world, and your research skills will be somewhat limited. This limits the degree to which you may put your participants at risk. If you go on to postgraduate study, you are likely to have more freedom, but you are also expected to have more skills and finesse, which will allow you to add to an existing body of knowledge. It may seem unfair, but that balance needs to be kept in mind.

In addition to the BPS Code, and any other formal code that may apply to you, you will also be influenced by your normative ethical principles (Mertins and Ginsberg, 2009). These are the internal ethical values and norms that are fundamental to your own perspective on what is right or wrong. Think about your own experiences throughout your life; these may well strongly influence how you think about the world. But they will also make you sensitive to certain things that others may not appreciate as being sensitive. It could be something very serious; you could have lost a close family member in a very sudden and traumatic way. Or it could be something less serious that you may think of as trivial – for example, eating habits. Asking questions about eating can be a very problematic area for some participants: they may have had an eating disorder, and they may have a very difficult relationship with food. When you design research, you need to try to anticipate the potential emotional impact of your research.

Task — When we think about ethics, we have to remember that not everyone will recognise our ethical code as being sufficient, or may even think it is too exhaustive. The ethics code is developed by recognising these differences and evaluating what changes need to be made.

— Can you think of something that is missing from the code of ethics?

Origins of the ethics code

How did the code of ethics that we now use come about? In the early days of psychology, there were fewer constraints on research practice. You can, undoubtedly, think of numerous early studies that would no longer be allowed – the Little Albert study, for example. The idea of even asking an ethics committee to approve a proposal for research that will scare and instil phobias in children would now seem unthinkable.

Before the Second World War, there were no profession-wide ethical guidelines. Institutions were free to impose ethical codes, or not, as they saw fit. During the Second World War, experiments were carried out on inmates of concentration camps. It was not until the camps were liberated that the extent of the horrific experiments was discovered. The Nuremberg War Trials Court prosecuted numerous members of the Third Reich. The evidence of the experiments led to the Nuremberg code, published in 1948, which set out a ten-point code of ethics to be used in experimentation that uses human participants. This formed the basis of the codes of ethics that now exist for medical and psychological research. The Nuremberg code set out the responsibilities of the experimenter – that the researcher should keep in mind the participants' welfare, the risks of the study must not outweigh the potential benefits of it, and experimenters should not attempt to engage in studies beyond their abilities. Although the Nuremberg code is over 60 years old, when you read the BPS ethical code, you will see that it remains at the heart of the code. Since the publication of the Nuremberg code, there have been later codes and declarations that have added to the guidelines that steer us in the ethics of our practice. The United Nations Declaration of Human Rights, also published in 1948, sets out the inalienable rights to dignity and self-determination. Even with these codes of practice, medical ethics scandals have occurred, and have further impacted upon what we do. It is noticeable that when you read about these they will sound shocking because our normative ethical principles have shifted in the intervening years. A good example of this is the Tuskegee syphilis study (Jones, 1981). This was carried out in the southern states of the USA from the 1930s to the 1970s. The American Public Health Service carried out a study on poor, black Americans, some of whom had syphilis, and some of whom did not. Participants were told that they were being enrolled on to a programme to treat their syphilis, but the aim of the programme was to examine the course of syphilis to the death of the sufferer. Syphilis is a disease that can result, in its final stages, in serious mental illness and dysfunction, until it ultimately kills the sufferer. Penicillin was found to be effective at treating syphilis in the 1940s, but despite a large volume of data being successfully collected, patients were not treated, and were in some cases actively dissuaded from seeking treatment elsewhere. It was only when the study was discovered in 1972 by uninvolved medical practitioners that the study was halted and the remaining participants were offered treatment. Individuals were also experimented on at the British military research facility at Porton Down. While most of the work that has been carried out there has been both ethical and very important, there have been a number of incidences of military personnel being experimented on without their full consent. Soldiers were told that they were engaging in studies into conditions such as the common cold, but were actually being used in studies of chemical weapons and nerve agents, such as sarin. Deaths have been linked to these experiments, and only after many years was the liability of the Ministry of Defence admitted. Scandals like these are met with anger and horror by the public, who may consequently lose confidence in researchers and choose not to participate in legitimate studies. As such, scandals have had a major impact on the code of ethics.

The code today

The BPS code of ethics has been developed around a number of core principles. These are respect, competence, responsibility and integrity. Each of these aspects is described as *a statement of values, reflecting the fundamental beliefs that guide ethical reasoning, decision making, and behaviour* (BPS Code of Ethics, p9). This statement is important because it states that ethics is not just a set of boxes we have to tick, but rather a way of thinking and a set of values that should guide us in research that involves others. In order to gain a better understanding of each of these four aspects, we will go through them one by one. You will see that the four aspects overlap in some areas, but that they come together to form the ethics code that regulates the research and practice of all psychologists.

Central principles

The BPS code of ethics states that we need to *respect* the participant – their feelings, well-being, beliefs and values. It helps if you put yourself in the position of the participant. Would you be happy to do this experiment, or be asked to answer these questions? The BPS guidelines also cover *informed consent*, which is one of the most important items. Do your participants have enough information about your experiment to give consent or are you going to spring something on them that they would have otherwise not consented to do? Informed consent requires that your participants fully understand what they are getting themselves into. Participants should be able to make an informed decision as to whether or not they participate in the study. This includes the requirement that you answer any questions concerning what might happen if they refuse to participate or withdraw from the study openly and responsibly. Participants should not be made to feel that there are any adverse consequences of their decision not to take part or complete their participation.

In many universities there are schemes that are in place to encourage students to participate in psychology studies and also provide a pool of participants for students and academics to draw upon when carrying out research. Students are encouraged to engage in a specified minimum amount of participation. You may well have taken part in such a scheme, and may intend to use the participant pool in your own research project. But there is a potential problem with these schemes: could it be argued that this is a form of coercion? Possibly, students may feel that they need to participate in studies that they are rather unsure about as they are running out of time to meet their required time commitment, and that if they don't it may mean that they have to take an extra assessment, or are refused the use of the participation scheme in their future studies.

There are times when informed consent is problematic. You may want your participants to be unaware of, or naive towards, to the aims of research. You will need to use a certain amount of *deception* or, in lay terms, withhold information from your participants. For example, there is a programme called Cyberball, which appears to be a multiplayer computer game that requires cooperation between players. The settings can be *manipulated* to make it seem that the other 'players' are shunning the participant. It is used to engender a feeling of social isolation in a participant (compare van Beest and Williams, 2006; Williams, 2007). If you were to tell your participants, it would spoil the effect of the experiment. So what do you do in research like this? You explain the research to the participants after the experiment. This is called *debriefing* and it is vital when any form of deception or withholding data has been used.

As well as giving participants the choice to participate, another vital aspect of ethics is maintaining participants' *right to withdraw*. This means that participants have the ability to change their minds during, or even after, the data gathering. Remember, just because someone has said 'yes, I'll do your study' it does not mean that they are under any requirement to complete that participation. So how does this work in practice? It is vital that participants understand that they can say 'stop' at any point and that the experimenter will respect this decision. It might be because the participant feels uncomfortable with the questions you are asking them, or because they are having a reaction to the experiment they are taking part in. To give you an example, when I was a student, I took part in a visual attention experiment. Most of my year group took part in the experiment, and were perfectly happy with it, but I have a visual deficit that, in combination with the experiment, made me feel horribly nauseous. The researchers could have had no idea that their design would have this effect on me, but I was made very aware that I could stop at any time, and it would not have any adverse effects for me. When you design a study, you need to think about the participants, and how to make sure they know that they can withdraw. The right to withdraw seems obvious to us, when we are looking from the outside, but it is important to remember that participants do not always feel able to say that they want to withdraw, and in reality, the very nature of participation in research can make people feel that they have to complete the study. A famous example of this is Milgram's (1963, 1974) experiments investigating obedience. In this study, participants were asked to apparently give increasingly strong electric shocks to another participant when they failed a learning task. Participants were told at the start of the experiment that they could withdraw. However, during the experiment when the participants said that they did not want to continue, the experimenter would respond by telling the participants they were to continue. Curiously, although the participants were told originally that they could withdraw, once in the experiment and being told to continue, 65 per cent of participants did so, involving apparently giving a fatal 450-volt shock. Milgram's experiments show that the experience of being in an experimental situation can be very persuasive.

When you are carrying out questionnaire studies, a slightly different aspect of the right to withdraw can occur. Participants can, and often do, fail to complete questionnaires. This can create problems, especially when you are left with partially completed questionnaires, or the number of people who have agreed to complete questionnaires seems much larger than the number of completed questionnaires with which you end up. A curious contradiction also presents itself with question-naires: if participants are given the right to withdraw, how do you maintain confidentiality?

Psychology research can often include collecting some very intimate and private information about participants. This is particularly common in qualitative research where we carry out interviews and focus groups. When we carry out such research, it is vital that we respect our participants' confidentiality, and keep their data private. If we gather data that might make our participants recognisable, we must ensure that identifying information is removed or *anonymised* when we write our reports. That means that when someone reads the report they cannot identify the individual.

Task

As you have read, sometimes we can deceive our participants and debrief them afterwards.

- Can you think of a situation where it would be justified to deceive your participants and to delay debriefing for a few days?

Competence and responsibility

In the BPS ethics code, the principle of competence relates primarily to practitioners such as clinical psychologists. Even though much of this does not seem to relate to you as a student, there are aspects that you need to take on board.

First, and probably most importantly, you must take responsibility for your actions, and you should act in a competent and ethical manner. It is not enough to say 'I didn't know I couldn't do that'; you must make sure that what you are doing is ethically correct. You need to make sure that you are competent in what you are doing. It is very tempting, when you think about the array of exciting equipment and tests that your department holds, to imagine the fantastic research you could do. The issue is how competent you are in the use of that equipment. Do you know how to use an EEG system? I certainly don't! So it is not a good idea to create a proposal that requires you to use one.

The *protection* of participants should be paramount during your research. You should try to ensure that they are not going to come to any harm, physically or psychologically, through participating in your research. You can probably think of research designs that could be informative, and possibly quite exciting, but that would be potentially harmful to the participants. The principle of protection means that you may need to be imaginative when designing your research. You may want to look at how people respond to cognitive tasks while they are in pain. Obviously, you cannot inflict pain in lasting or damaging ways, so what could you do in this case? Well, one way of causing transitory pain is to ask participants to hold ice or put their hand into ice-cold water. Try it yourself – it is quite painful – but as soon as you let go of the ice, or take your hand out of the water you feel better (obviously, you don't have contact with the ice for very long). Using this method, you can induce pain, but the participant retains control and is able to stop as soon as they want to.

Another aspect of competence is not to overstep your ability in the field of psychology. You are not a qualified diagnostician, so you must not offer diagnosis or *advice*. This also means that you cannot, nor should you offer to, tell people about their personality or anything else that you may be testing. While you and your friends may have great fun doing informal quizzes that claim to be able to tell you about yourself, when you are doing something with the validity of a psychological study, you should treat the tests with great respect. Indeed, providing misleading or incomplete information or misrepresenting yourself may upset or confuse participants. It is, however, good ethical practice to offer information about sources of support and further information relating to participants' concerns that may have been triggered by taking part in the study. An example can be provided by studies investigating the experience of bereavement. While it would be unethical to recruit people who have experienced a recent loss, the study may still elicit strong emotions after any period of bereavement. In this situation, you would need to provide contact details for organisations that can provide professional support if it is needed.

In addition to ensuring that you do not try to do something you are not really competent to do, it is vital that you take responsibility for the safety of your participants. For example, if your participant is becoming visibly upset, you should try to both calm and reassure them and, if necessary, stop the interview or experiment. It is not enough to just complete the experiment, task or interview; you need to ensure that the participant does not become distressed.

Responsibility means that we must take responsibility for our actions, but also that we must take responsibility of care for our participants and the data that we collect from them. Our participants are very generous, both with their time and with what they are prepared to do for us. Sometimes the material gathered is perfectly innocuous, but it often contains potentially sensitive information. Because of this, we need to maintain *confidentiality* of data. This means that we keep the data private and secure, and that participants cannot be identified from their data. With questionnaire studies this can be quite simple; we ask participants not to put any identifying material on the questionnaire, such as name or date of birth. However, if your study requires repeat measures or an experiment, you need to be able to identify participants' data. This can be done by using a combination of numbers and letters that the participant can easily recall. Try not to use the participants' initials and date of birth, for obvious reasons. Some researchers use a more imaginative combination, including letters from a participant's mother's name, the first numbers of their home phone number, things like that. As you will see, qualitative data with identifying information is anonymised, but clearly the original data is not going to be anonymised, so it is important that it is kept securely, preferably in a password-protected file. This has become much easier since the introduction of digital data-recording; it was much more challenging when data was captured on cassette tape!

Integrity

If you read the BPS code of conduct, you might think that the *integrity* section does not really seem to apply to you. It is true that a lot of this section is concerned with the integrity of psychologists who are in clinical practice, and the ways that they should work with their clients and/or patients. However, the integrity section also includes some very important guidance for all psychologists, whether they are professionals, academics or students. This revolves around a single important principle: we should tell the truth. We should be truthful in our writing; this covers both plagiarism and acknowledgements. If you try to present someone else's work as your own it is dishonest and is classed as plagiarism. This would be a breach of the principle of integrity. If someone helps you, you should acknowledge this in your report and thank them. Have a look at the front of some of your textbooks and you will see acknowledgement of colleagues who advised on the writing and the author's family, who put up with them during the writing. Also, if someone is funding your research, for example a research council or a commercial company, then you should acknowledge that. After all, you would want to know whether the study you are reading, which states how useful chewing gum is in helping you concentrate, is funded by a chewing gum manufacturer.

Other considerations

Animal studies

The use of non-human animals in research is not as common today as it once was, but it is still an important field of research. In your studies you have probably read some pretty horrible accounts of experiments on *non-human animals*, so we will not recount them here. Years ago, under-graduates would engage in experiments with rats and frogs, but you are very unlikely to be asked to do this today. Researchers who use non-human animals in their research are governed by both a strict set of ethical principles set out by the BPS and by laws relating to the scientific use of animals (Animals (Scientific Procedures) Act, 1986). Institutions that engage in this kind of research have to hold a Home Office licence, and are routinely inspected to ensure that they are meeting the requirements of the licence. To be able to use non-human animals, researchers must be able to show that the research cannot be carried out by any other means, the harm caused to the animals must be kept to an absolute minimum, and the potential benefits must outweigh any harm or distress to the animals involved.

Research for which you cannot obtain informed consent

The kinds of work for which you are unlikely to be able to get full consent are studies that use naturally occurring data in public spaces. These include *observational* studies. You might be observing how shoppers react in a large shopping mall, how they move around and what they do. Think about the news footage that you see every year of shoppers who have queued overnight for the big sales, and how they react once the shop doors are opened. This kind of research is interesting as it gives an insight into crowd behaviour, which we could not get with an artificially created environment. There are, however, certain restrictions on this kind of research. Even in a public space, you still have a reasonable expectation of privacy. This means that you would not expect to be observed in certain places, such as public toilets, changing rooms or public telephones. Researchers should ensure that they respect this expectation of privacy. Observation studies may seem fairly harmless, but they have raised controversies in the past. One of the most shocking examples was known as the tearoom trade study (Humphrey, 1970). In this study, men were observed engaging in homosexual activities in public toilets (an activity known as tearooming in the USA, and cottaging in the UK). The men were not only observed taking part in sexual activities, but some of them were then traced through their car registration numbers. They were also interviewed under the guise of 'health research' studies and asked details about their life, work and marital status. At the time that this study was conducted, homosexuality still carried a high risk of public shaming and possible prosecution. The participants were undertaking the activities in a public place, but they were given no opportunity to withdraw and were not fully informed. The study, understandably, caused huge upset when it was published, and it continues to be used to illustrate bad practice in observation and ethnographic studies today.

When you go into lots of public areas today, you are probably aware that you are being observed by CCTV. Equally, when you phone a call centre you are likely to be told that your call 'may be recorded for training or other purposes'. The data gathered from CCTV and call centres may be used for research purposes, and it has become such a day-to-day part of our lives, we often do not even notice it. What this does mean is that we spend much more of our time being in observed situations than we ever did before, but we should not take it for granted that the potential to use the data for research purposes is entirely without ethical problems.

Another semi-public place is the internet. You may well use social networking sites, and communicate with many people in that way. But this is also an area where we often forget how public things actually are. Pictures and comments on Facebook that have been posted, apparently for the users' friends, have had serious repercussions for the person or people involved. The internet is not, despite appearances, a private space. In many ways, the internet presents a boundless supply of rich data and data-gathering opportunities for psychologists. Psychologists have already started to use social networking sites as both sources of data and as an object of research in itself. This does not mean that you can just go ahead and use material from the internet as your data set. You must remember that the website owner retains copyright on the site, and so permission must be sought from the site owner before data can be used. Also, if you want to use data from message boards, it is ethically good practice not only to gain permission from the site owner, but also to post to let users know that you are intending to use data from the message board. This will allow site users to state that they do not want their data included.

Another interesting opportunity that the internet has presented is the potential to gather participants and even to administer questionnaires and experiments via the internet. While this looks like a fantastic idea, it does present problems. How sure can you be that your participants are giving informed consent and that they feel able to withdraw? As this is such a new area of research, the ethics covering it are also very new, and most institutions will have their own policies until the BPS provide greater guidance. Remember, just because data is in a public (or semi-) public domain does not mean that you have carte blanche to use it.

Who is protected?

You might well think that the ethical code exists only to protect research participants. A more accurate perspective would be that the code also protects researchers and the institutions to which they are affiliated. If you can say that you have adhered to the ethical code, and that the study has been approved by the ethics committee, you have done everything that you can to protect the participant and your own reputation. After all, you have taken the time to ensure that the research will not cause harm; the participant must know what they are getting themselves into and be able to withdraw at any time. But is that sufficient? Is it enough to say 'I've ticked the boxes, so I've protected the participants'?

When we design studies, would it not be better to be more active in considering ethics? For example, you could say, 'Well, I'm not doing anything that the ethics code says I shouldn't do, so surely that's fine?' That would be fine; you would pass the ethics committee, and make a start on your data collection. However, maybe it would be better to say, 'How would I feel about doing this if I, or someone I know, was a participant?' The ethics code is constantly adapting and evolving, and things we can do today are somewhat different from what our predecessors could do 50 years ago. Among the things that affect these changes is our own practice of ethics; our critical interpretation of what constitutes ethics also changes.

The grey areas

When you read the code of ethics, it discusses participants with whom you need to take extra care. This primarily concerns vulnerable groups, such as small children or people with profound mental impairments. The principle is that those who cannot make a clear rational decision regarding the intricacies of the research should not be asked to give their 'informed' consent to participate in it. However, the code stipulates child participants as being under 18. If the participants are seven years old, it is obvious that they will have difficulty giving informed consent, but think about participants at the upper end of that age scale. A participant who is 17 may feel perfectly capable of giving consent, and may feel aggrieved at having to ask for parental permission. You can overcome this by ensuring that you have the consent of both the participant and their parent or guardian, but you need to be prepared to get a rejection from one party if they think it is unsuitable. An example can be provided by the study of sexual behaviour among adolescents and the rate of STDs among this group. From a legal perspective, the participants are all able to give consent to sex, and their sexual health matters are confidential from their parents. Asking questions about sexual behaviour, sexuality and sexual health is a sensitive area, and potential participants may not want their parents to know anything about it, but the code of ethics dictates that you need to gain permission. What do you think the ethics committee would decide and what sort of compromise might they accept? It is grey areas like this that raise serious ethical concerns.

Another grey area occasionally appears in qualitative studies: serendipitous data. Serendipitous data is information that arises during data collection that was not originally part of the investigation. For example, in a research study that was collecting recordings of family conversations over a long period of time, one of the participants was diagnosed with terminal cancer. The researchers asked if the family would like to withdraw, but they chose to continue. As a result, the researchers were able to gain a unique data set – a family's day-to-day conversations as a member of the family was dying. This is a data set that would be almost impossible to gather in another way. It could be argued that participants who had just been told that they, or their loved one, had been diagnosed with a serious illness would not be able to give a truly informed consent.

Using data obtained by unethical means

As we have seen, data exists that we gain serendipitously, but there is another grey and problematic area that needs to be examined. Data exists that has been gained through unethical means. Researchers must decide whether to use that data while acknowledging the means by which it is gathered, or reject it, arguing that to use it is to tacitly approve of the means by which it has been collected. You will hear convincing arguments for both sides, and you may find yourself shifting from one position to another. That is not surprising; it is a question that tries the ethical and philosophical conscience. If we go back to the historical origins of the ethics code, we find a prime example. During the Second World War, Dr Sigmund Rascher carried out experiments on prisoners in Dachau concentration camp. He studied the effects of freezing temperatures on the human body. In the experiments, camp prisoners were systematically frozen to death, or close to death. Further experiments were carried out to determine how people could be revived, and the prisoners who were unconscious, but still alive, were heated by various means. Numerous concentration camp inmates were killed in these experiments, in tests that they were forced to be a part of with no respect for them as human beings. What was found was that people whose core temperature had dropped to a dangerous level could be revived by gradually raising their temperature. The experimentation carried out in concentration camps has provided most of our current understanding concerning how the human body reacts to extreme cold. The use of this data remains controversial and while lives have undoubtedly been saved as a result, the knowledge was gained through maiming and killing. Discussions of cases like this continue to exercise ethicists, and the ethics of using the findings of the experiments to help people remains a subject of debate.

You may well think, 'Well, I'm not likely to use that, so this won't really impact on my research'. Maybe research as extreme as this example will not be relevant to your own undergraduate experiments but other, less extreme cases have provided valuable lessons. In your Individual Differences studies, you will probably have come across the work of Cyril Burt, a highly respected researcher in the field of intelligence, particularly around the concept of the heritability of IQ. His work was influential in the development of the 11-plus test, which was fundamental to education in Britain after the Second World War. His work relied on an enormous number of monozygotic twins. However, after his death, doubts were raised as to the legitimacy of his data, and claims were made that he had fabricated some of his findings. This was made even more problematic by the fact that his original data was destroyed after his death, so verifying the data is impossible. The debate continues today, and his defenders claim that he has been unfairly accused and that his work remains entirely legitimate. His critics claim that his work is irrevocably compromised by the false data, and so his work should not be used as the foundation for study or policy. The debate about this is also coloured by different perspectives on heritability of IQ, so this is one of those arguments that is not entirely straightforward. You can read impassioned arguments from both sides, and it is up to you to decide where you sit on the 'Burt Affair' (Gould, 1981). What this does highlight is the question of using data that may be compromised. Clearly, much of Burt's data set is entirely genuine, so even if you do not agree with his position, it is data that can be used. However, if you accept that some of the data is potentially fabricated, can or should any data or conclusions drawn from them be used?

Critical thinking activity

Using ethically problematic data

Critical thinking focus: reflection

Key question: *Should we use data that has been gathered unethically?*

You have just read about the debates regarding ethically problematic data. The question as to whether you should use data that was gathered unethically is a personal decision. However, your position should be carefully thought about and justified, rather than being a simple emotional response. This activity requires you to reflect on the debate and come to your own conclusions as to what extent we can use problematic data.

Consider the following to aid your reflection.

- As the data have already been used, does this mean that they have already been validated?

- Can we expect that all of the data gathered in the past meets the contemporary code of ethics?

- Do the potential benefits of the research outweigh the ethical problems?

- We know that some data are ethically unsound or fabricated, but to what extent can we have total confidence about other data?

Critical thinking review

This activity helps you to develop your skills in reflecting upon ethical practices and deliberating about ethical dilemmas. If ethical decisions were a simple matter this chapter would have been a lot shorter.

Your own position on the use of ethically problematic data is going to be a very personal response, and you will need to develop your own arguments to support your position. The skill in reflecting on your own opinion and developing an academic argument to support that opinion is vital throughout your studies.

You may feel that the use of all such data is illegitimate, and the theories based on the results are irrevocably compromised. If this is the case, and keeping in mind the interconnectedness of much psychological research, how much of our body of knowledge needs to be consigned to the scrap heap?

On the other hand, you may feel that the data exists, and not using it will not right any of the wrongs of gathering the data, so it should be used. If so, at what point does data become unusable? How badly should the ethics code be breached before you say that the data should be rejected?

Skill builder activity

Making ethics decisions

Transferable skill focus: problem solving

Key question: *How do you work in the grey areas of consent?*

You intend to carry out research that needs to use participants between 16 and 18 years old. You want to ask them about their understanding of sexually transmitted diseases, but you know that your participants are under the age of consent according to the BPS guidelines. How might you go about gaining consent, while still encouraging your participants to be as open as possible?

Skill builder review

The problem of using participants in the 16- to 18-year-old age bracket is clear. While you need to gain parental consent, you do not want to alienate your participants by telling them they need to do something because their parent or guardian has said they can. It may be useful to consider how you would have reacted to the idea of being volunteered for such research at that age. You could think about using an internet-mediated research tool to gather data, but then you still have the problem of consent and you cannot guarantee that all of your participants are the correct age. You might find that a better solution would be to ask consent of both the responsible adult and the young person themselves. By doing this, you can maintain your adherence to the ethics code, but you are also respecting the autonomy of your potential participant.

Assignments

1. To what extent did early unethical research contribute towards the development of a coherent and universal code of ethics? Discuss with reference to contemporary research.

2. Critically evaluate the claim that data collected through unethical means may still be insightful and used to test or elaborate theories in psychology.

3. Critically discuss the pros and cons of adhering to the BPS code of ethics with reference to investigating socially sensitive phenomena.

4. To what extent have the BPS ethical guidelines protected vulnerable groups while still facilitating the study of complex social phenomena and the extension of knowledge?

Summary: what you have learned

This chapter has introduced you to ethical issues surrounding research. You should have some awareness of the different elements of the current ethics code, as well as an understanding of ethics as a dynamic process.

You should also have an awareness of the debates within ethics. This includes the problem of using potentially unethical data and determining which groups are considered to be vulnerable participants who require greater protection. These areas are also fluctuating, and we all need to keep up with the changes debates in these areas.

Now you have read this chapter and completed the exercises, you should feel more confident in your understanding of both using and debating ethics. The tasks should also have helped you to develop your reflection and problem-solving skills. These skills will be very important in your psychology studies, and also in your ability to develop your own research projects.

Further reading

British Psychological Society (2009) *BPS Code of Ethics and Conduct*. Available online at www.bps. org.uk/the-society/code-of-conduct/code-of-conduct_home.cfm [Accessed 2 April 2011]

It is worth making yourself familiar with the code – it will be used throughout your psychology studies.

Gould, SJ (1981) *The Mismeasure of Man*. London: Norton and Company.

This book tackles the issues around measuring intelligence and the potential biases that can arise while assessing populations. It also has a section that deals with the 'Burt Affair' and is highly critical of this approach.

Humphrey, L (1970) *Tearoom Trade: A Study of Homosexual Encounters in Public Places*. London: Duckworth.

This is an example of how earlier research often broke participants' rights to privacy, information and the right to withdraw.

Jones, H (1981) *Bad Blood: The Tuskegee Syphilis Experiment*. New York: Free Press.

This is an example of how perspectives have changed over time and a demonstration of how unethical practices can be harmful.

Mertins, D and Ginsberg, P (2009) *The Handbook of Social Research Ethics*. London: Sage.

This is pretty much the bible of research ethics in the social sciences. Mertins and Ginsberg's book covers a vast area of ethics, including philosophy and applications of ethics.

Milgram, S (1963) Behavioral Study of Obedience. *Journal of Abnormal and Social Psychology*, 67(4), 371–378.

This is the original article concerning Milgram's infamous obedience experiments.

Milgram, S (1974) *Obedience to Authority: An Experimental View*. London: HarperCollins.

This is a detailed and critical review of Milgram's study into obedience.

van Beest, I and Williams, KD (2006) When inclusion costs and ostracism pays, ostracism still hurts. *Journal of Personality and Social Psychology*, 91, 918–928.

This is a study of ostracism and inclusion. Even when given financial incentives to be ostracised, this was still a negative experience.

Weindling, PJ (2006) *Nazi Medicine and the Nuremberg Trials: From Medical War Crimes to Informed Consent*. London: Palgrave Macmillan.

This gives an account of the War Crimes Trials and the experimentation carried out in Nazi concentration camps. It discusses how this led to the ethical guidelines we have today. While this is a harrowing read, it is also fascinating.

Williams, KD (2007) Ostracism. *Annual Review of Psychology*, 58, 425–445.

This is another paper reviewing the effects of ostracism.

Chapter 3

Levels of measurement

Learning outcomes

The purpose of this chapter is to introduce you to one of the fundamental bases of quantitative research: measuring stuff! Two prominent categories of measurement are presented, and the concept of errors in measurements is discussed. This is vital in order to ensure you develop a firm understanding of how to cultivate good research practice, but also to appreciate the implications for the subsequent analysis of data derived from your studies.

By the end of this chapter you should:

- *be able to identify the four levels of measurement;*

- *understand the differences between discrete and continuous variables;*

- *be aware of the concept of errors in measurement;*

- *have developed your critical and creative thinking skills;*

- *have practised your problem-solving skills.*

Introduction

Measurement can be defined as *the assignment of numerals to objects and events according to rule* (Stevens, 1946, p677). Conducting research is a fundamental step in improving your knowledge of any given topic. Researchers are interested in specific behaviours, events or constructs, and wish to develop theories concerning these. In order to achieve this, the first necessary step is to define and then measure the things to be investigated. Should these measurements be poorly executed, then the research quickly flounders and we have learned nothing concerning our **variables** of interest.

A variable is simply some property of an event or person that will have different values at different times, depending on the conditions. By **quantifying** these different levels within a variable, it is then possible to measure the extent of changes to this variable. During an experiment, we systematically control and manipulate one variable in order to determine if this has a systematic effect on a second variable (our behaviour of interest) by measuring the changes in its values. This, in turn, allows us to learn about cause-and-effect relationships by the use of quantitative measures. In short, learning how to measure variables is a key step in good research practice. This is a straightforward account – you will learn later on that a multitude of variables can be both manipulated and/or measured simultaneously in a single experiment.

First steps

As an example, suppose you are interested in the impulsivity levels of people with antisocial personality disorder. First you need to operationalise the term impulsiveness (i.e. define what you mean) in order to make any predictions or hypotheses. You may consider impulsiveness to be failing to plan ahead, making very quick decisions, giving up quickly on tasks, or possibly some other characteristic. Once you have decided upon the definition of your variable, you then need to decide how to measure this variable.

At first glance, this may seem to be a rather simplistic and downright obvious step. However, while the term 'measuring' may immediately conjure up images of someone with a ruler systematically measuring something physically tangible and present, such as a table, in psychology we often wish to measure things that are not corporeal. For instance, we may wish to measure theoretical constructs such as someone's intelligence, personality or level of anxiety. In cases such as these, we obviously cannot measure something that is intangible and so we need to infer variable levels of these constructs based on how they perform on our measures. Returning to our previous example of impulsiveness, we may wish to use a questionnaire to determine how impulsive our participants are. Alternatively, we may decide to employ a behavioural task such as the 'go/no go' test in order to reveal this (see Rubia et al., 2007 for an explanation of this and other tests of impulsivity). Should participants score highly on the questionnaire, or happen to make more commission errors on the behavioural task, we can then infer levels of impulsivity and compare the performance scores to those of others.

Thus the types of assessments and tasks typically used in psychological research do not directly measure the variable of interest. Even biological measures, such as skin conductance rates, EEG recordings or fMRI signals, are only indirect measures of whichever theoretical construct (such as anxiety) is being tested. Due to this issue, you will notice that there is a plethora of instruments, tasks and scales, all of which purport to measure the very same construct. It should quickly become apparent that some measures are better than others.

Levels of measurement

As you can probably tell, the different instruments available to measure some variables are not homogeneous. They possess different properties or **levels of measurement** that can be delineated according to an increasing level of complexity (Stevens, 1946). Principally these include:

- nominal;

- ordinal;

- interval;

- ratio.

It is necessary to understand the differences in these measurement levels as they dictate what kind of statistical analysis you may wish to conduct on the data collected from your research. However, it is important to note that this classification scheme proposed by Stevens (1946) is not universally accepted, nor is it the only conceptualisation of measurement. Other classification schemes do exist (for example, Luce and Tukey, 1964; Luce et al., 1990) but are beyond the scope of this introductory textbook. Suffice to say that there is criticism of Stevens' classification scheme based on its failure to adequately describe the attributes of certain data; quite often data may appear to possess features of more than one of the specified four levels, and is often a source of disagreement between research methods staff! Michell (1997) appears to be particularly critical, arguing that psychology *has its own definition of measurement . . . quite unlike the traditional concept used in the physical sciences* (p360). For a useful introduction to these critiques, we recommend you read the commentary by Velleman and Wilkinson (1993).

Nominal levels of measurement are the most basic and simplest form – they refer to variables that reflect categories. For instance, let us say you wanted to find out how your friends voted at the last general election. The choices on offer (i.e. Labour, Conservative, Liberal Democrat, other or none) are **exhaustive** – these five options cover all possible scenarios and so any response from your friends can be assigned to a **category**. For instance, any vote for the three main parties would be assigned to the respective category; however, if any of your friends happened to vote for the SNP, UKIP or an independent candidate, this would be included under the 'other' category; if a friend abstained from voting or was indisposed for some reason (ill, on holiday or detained at Her Majesty's pleasure), then this would come under the 'none' category. Other features of categories include their **exclusive** and discrete properties – your friends can only vote for one of these options; they cannot vote for more than one party at the same election. Nor can they place their voting cross at some midway point between these political categories and vote for some chimerical blend of candidate (though people do argue it is difficult to tell one politician from the other!).

Task —

Perhaps a clearer example of the exhaustive, exclusive and discrete property of categories is being pregnant. You either are or are not pregnant – there is no other option, nor can you be both at the same time, and similarly you cannot be a bit pregnant!

– Can you think of a similar variable?

Typically, if we wish to analyse nominal data (statistically speaking) we need to enter these categories into a computer software program (typically, this is SPSS but there are others). Due to the vagaries of software, you need to stipulate that these categories are distinct from each other and this is achieved by assigning numerical codes to each category (for example, 1 for Labour, 2 for Conservative, 3 for Liberal Democrat and so forth). Don't let this confuse you – these codes are merely labels and have no inherent numerical value. It doesn't mean that the Labour candidate is worth less than the others, or that the Liberal Democrat candidate is better than the Conservative. Unfortunately, when some students first start using data analysis software they usually include categorical variables (such as the sex of participants: 1 for male and 2 for female) in their descriptive analyses in order to find the mean average. Quite often they may determine the mean sex to be 1.48 but, of course, this figure is meaningless.

The actual scores from nominal data that we are interested in analysing refer to the size of individual categorical membership. You can add up and total the number of people who voted for each particular party – and that is just about all you can do! The numbers we have obtained (or said to have been observed) refer to a simple frequency count. By analysing the differences between the observed and expected frequencies of categories (i.e. when we expect there to be an equal share of the votes between the political parties), it is possible to determine if this difference is statistically significant.

Ordinal levels are the next step up in complexity. These variables are still based on categories, but offer the distinct advantage of being able to be **rank-ordered** according to specific criteria. The ascending (or descending) nature of these ranks can then formally indicate whether one score is

Table 3.1: Summary classification of measurement according to Stevens (1946)

	Level of measurement	Explanation
Increasing level of complexity	Nominal	Variables refer to discrete categories and is measured in frequency (counts) of membership. *For example, number of people who voted Labour, Conservative or Lib Dem at the last election.*
	Ordinal	Scores can be ranked according to some criterion. *For example, performance in an exam may be graded as a fail, pass, merit, credit or distinction.*
	Interval	Differences in measurement scale are equidistant. *For example, 10°C is 2°C warmer than 8°C – this difference is the same as that between 36°C and 34°C.*
	Ratio	This level has ratios between scores on the scale and a non-arbitrary zero value. *For example, 0cm indicates zero length; 1.3m is twice as long as 0.65m.*

worth more than another. For example, suppose children take part in an egg and spoon race and you record the places in which they finished (first, second, third, fourth and so on). We know that first place is better than second place (it is intrinsically worth more) and that fourth is of lower value than third place; however, we do not know how much better the difference is in these positions, only that the difference echoes some sense of having more or less value. To clarify, we have no inkling of how much quicker the child who came first was in contrast to the child in second place – they may have won by a hair's breadth (and only had this revealed courtesy of a photo-finish), or they may have romped home by a country mile. There is no way to determine this with ordinal measures; instead, we would need to engage a more complex level of measurement.

Interval level measures also reflect that test scores can give an overall indication of performance in terms of higher or lower ability. However, what sets them apart from an ordinal measure is that it is possible to infer a degree of **magnitude** when observing a difference in scores on a task (see Chapter 11). A typical example of an interval measure is a thermometer that uses the Fahrenheit, Centigrade or Celsius scale – these scales are composed of degree intervals that are of equal size wherever you look up and down on the thermometer. A 1°C interval on the scale has exactly the same value at any other juncture on the scale. For instance, the difference between 22°C and 23°C is exactly the same as the difference between 35°C and 36°C further up the scale. Another illustration would be performance on a test of general intelligence – the 10-point difference between getting 35/50 and 45/50 correct is exactly the same as the 10-point gap between getting 12/50 and 22/50 correct. It is this use of intervals on the scale that now permits the inference of comparisons between scores on such tasks.

However, interval measures do not possess an absolute zero value. While answering 0/50 correct on a test of general intelligence may look pretty bad, this zero is artificial. It does not mean that the person has a complete lack of intelligence, just that they failed to score on that particular test. It could be that the test was so difficult it precipitated a floor effect and everyone scored poorly. Similarly, 0°C on a thermometer does not mean there is an absence of temperature: 0°C still registers as a temperature as the scale can extend beyond this into the minus region. As a side note, the exception to this is the Kelvin scale of temperature – this was created intentionally to possess an absolute zero and it is not possible to go any colder than this figure (if you are interested, zero (0K) on the Kelvin scale is equivalent to -273.15°C.

Ratio levels of measurement have all the features of interval levels, but do possess an absolute zero value. With ratio levels, it is possible to genuinely score nothing. Classic examples of ratio measures are time (for example, 0 hours spent revising for exams), length (to record 0mm growth in height over a one-month period), weight (to lose 0kg while on a diet) or scores on a test (0/10 words spelled correctly). An advantage of this zero value is that it permits the calculation of ratios among the scoring scale. For instance, a child who scored 8/10 on a spelling test got twice as many correct as someone who scored 4/10, and got four times as many correct as someone who scored 2/10.

At first glance, including performance on this spelling test as a ratio, measure may seem to contradict classifying the general intelligence test as interval (or arguably as ordinal). However, if we determine that the spelling test is only an indication of the number of correctly spelled words, it is possible to have 0/10 and so this is a ratio scale. Considering this as a test of linguistic ability would invalidate the absolute zero value, and we would have to question whether there are genuinely equal intervals between the scores (are the words equally difficult to spell?) and so therefore arguably make it ordinal.

Psychological tasks that feature this ratio level of measurement are few and far between. The reason for this is that these are direct measures of something tangible and physically present, but psychological research typically works with variables that are hypothetical constructs and can only be measured indirectly by inferring levels of ability from tests designed to assess them.

Task — What are the following levels of measurement?

   – Ice-cream sales.

   – Body temperature.

   – Political party affiliation.

   – FTSE 100 index.

Discrete versus continuous variables

A further division of variables is made on the basis of their units of measurement. As previously mentioned for nominal and ordinal variables, these variables are expressed in categories. The units of measurement (for example, voting preferences, favourite colour and pregnancy status) are **discrete** from each other; these are indivisible. It is not possible to have a more precise measure or have some mid-point score; they can be only whole number values (for example, 1 for Labour, 2 for Conservative, 3 for Lib Dem and so forth). Such measures have no mid-points or intervals in between the respective categories. As such there is no meaningful gap between first and second place (coming 1.5th in a race simply does not make sense). See Figure 3.1a to see how this can be plotted on a bar graph to emphasise the discrete nature of the variable.

Interval and ratio level measures, on the other hand, can be **continuous variables**. The unit of measurement can be divided (continually) into smaller and ever more precise units (see Figure 3.1b to see how a continuous variable is plotted with a line graph). For example, if we wanted to measure the distance someone could run before having to stop we could express this measure in terms of kilometres. However, they may stop at some point between 4 and 5km and so we need to be more precise – the kilometre could then be subdivided into increasingly smaller units

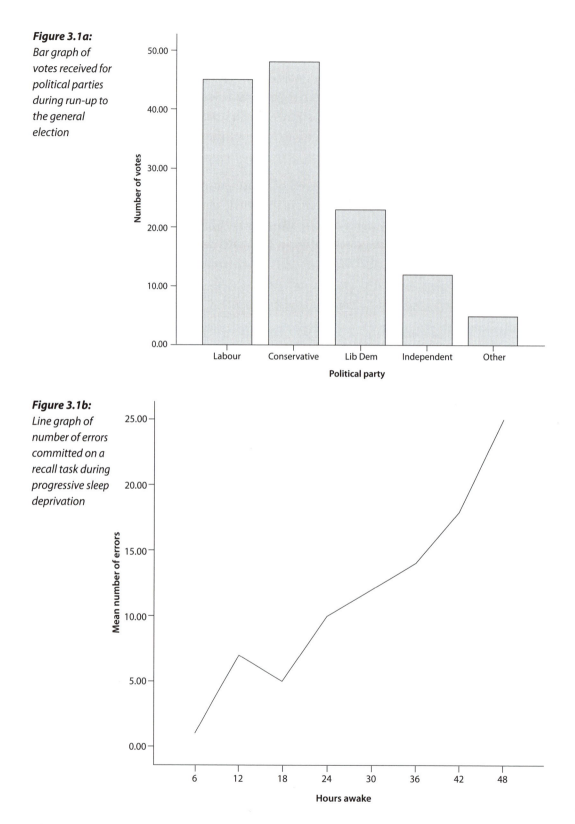

Figure 3.1a:
Bar graph of votes received for political parties during run-up to the general election

Figure 3.1b:
Line graph of number of errors committed on a recall task during progressive sleep deprivation

(metres). We could extend this subdivision infinitely, becoming increasingly accurate with each subdivision (km>m>cm>mm>$_{mu}$m>$_n$m>$_p$m and so on). However, this would be a pretty pointless and expensive exercise, unless you work in nuclear physics where I'd imagine being this accurate is somewhat more preferable! Instead, we would settle on an **approximate value** such as 4.56km. This is a far more practical and worthwhile endeavour, despite the fact we are now making a continuous variable discrete simply by virtue of measuring it!

The problem with measurement

Critics of the quantitative measures argue that the use of scales that quantify human experience fails to do what it sets out to do. Some measures are obvious and necessary – for example, the time it takes to respond to a stimulus in a cognitive experiment (a ratio level). But consider researched aspects of human experience that are not so fixed: how do you measure happiness, or love, or distress? If I ask you how sitting an exam makes you feel, you'll probably say stressed, but do you have the same level of stress as someone else on your course? Moreover, how is it possible to find out if you are experiencing it differently from your friend if all we have to go on is a set of pre-defined measures with which you can respond? What of your own subjective expressions and interpretation?

Another critique often levelled at quantitative measures is that, by their very nature, they are limited to conceptualising differences or similarities in terms of numerical changes only. They fail to deal with the 'why?' I may know two students, and they both get very stressed about exams. Lauren gets stressed because she has good grades, and she feels pressure to maintain them; Lindsay gets stressed because she knows she does not perform well in exams, but she needs to pass the exam with a high score in order to improve her grades. Asking Lauren and Lindsay how much they get stressed will give you a one-dimensional answer, but it cannot capture the difference in the two students' experiences. You could imply that the exam scores are a measure, but they do not necessarily reflect anything more than the students' performance on the day. When tutors mark exam papers and look at the overall marks for a module, we are aware of the context in which these exam results exist. For example, we know that one student may have got 52 per cent, but recall that they have struggled with the module and have worked hard at revising, and so we are pleased that they managed to achieve that grade. Another student gets 52 per cent and we are disappointed, because we know that they should have got a much better grade, but they were a bit complacent about the module. If we factor in the context, then we may have a qualitative insight into a student's strengths and limitations, which a pure numerical score will not reflect.

Errors in measurement

No matter how careful we may be with a ruler, or how thorough we were in creating a question-naire, any measure we use will always have a degree of error. The actual score that is observed (recorded) in a research study comprises the true score and some error term; this error term can affect the reliability and validity of your data, i.e. how consistent and meaningful your data and any conclusions drawn from it are (see Chapters 1 and 6 for a more detailed explanation of reliability and validity). Therefore, care should be taken to try to minimise the extent of any error in your measures.

These errors can appear randomly or systematically. Random error occurs when a measure is either too high or low at any one point in time. For example, as part of a biology practical assessment a class of students were asked to accurately measure the length of a leaf. Students were provided with a tape measure. It quickly became apparent that the reported measurements were all different – broadly, they were the same in terms of the nearest centimetre, but the assessment specified the measurement was to be in millimetres. In some cases the leaf had curled slightly due to the warmth of the room, and so some students started to stretch out the leaf while measuring it, thereby recording longer lengths; others did not and recorded shorter lengths. This introduced random error into the measurements. Fortunately, these random errors (positive and negative = long versus short) tend to balance themselves out and so overall maintain a degree of reliability (to the nearest centimetre in this instance).

A systematic error in a measure occurs when some constant value has been added or taken away from the measure. For example, my father-in-law is a joiner and once told me about how a workmate of his did not dig the foundations for a garage of sufficient depth to meet the building regulations. When the inspector arrived, he measured this and served notice that the hole was two inches too shallow and that the foundations would need digging deeper. Rather than go to the hassle of doing this, when the inspector next came out this workmate quickly cut the first two inches off his tape measure and thus the hole then appeared to meet the regulation depth. However, he continued to use this modified tape measure and subsequently was consistently measuring two inches short. By shortening his tape measure he had introduced a systematic error, which he failed to spot immediately! There is no balancing out of systematic errors and so overall these will result in measures that are consistently too high (or too low, depending on the direction of the error).

Task — Having an error in your measures may sound horrific, but this is to be expected. You need to try to minimise these errors beforehand.

– How might you do this?

Critical thinking activity

Measurement

Critical thinking focus: critical and creative thinking

Key question: *What does measuring really mean?*

The issue of measuring psychological variables should not be overlooked. To a psychologist with a quantitative background, this may seem to be a perfectly rational and straightforward process, but a critical appraisal of this venture is vital to appreciate what exactly is being undertaken.

Consider the following questions to aid your critical appraisal.

- Are all psychological variables genuinely quantitative?

- Are we imposing an objective scale on to subjective concepts such as beliefs, feelings, opinions and experiences?

- Are the four levels of measurement equally affected by this?

- Does putting a number on someone's personality have any meaning in the real world?

- If you think some variables are truly immeasurable, what properties do they possess that makes them so resistant to this process?

Play devil's advocate:

- How might you defend measuring someone's level of emotional intelligence to a sceptic?

- What possible benefit might repeated testing bestow?

Critical thinking review

This activity helps develop your skills of critical thinking and reflection in relation to the quantification and measuring of psychological variables. To do this, you were encouraged to consider if all psychological variables were genuinely quantitative, i.e. does assigning a number to something truly mean you have captured its value? Does one category mean the same for everyone? Might not 'strongly agree' for one person feel like 'strongly agree' for another? How is it possible to define the strength of feeling?

This is a common critique of quantitative measures – how can an artificially contrived scale possibly be imposed upon a given construct? You may have given thought to the phenomena that psychological variables *do* demonstrate predictive power and can be remarkably consistent and stable over time and repeated testing. If quantifying and measuring such constructs was totally meaningless and redundant, then this very consistency would not appear. Indeed, it is the very stability and consistency of such measures that supports the argument of quantification to be a valid and useful process.

This enabled you to think about the usefulness of quantitative measures in practice. Thinking critically about an issue, being able to understand both sides of a debate, and reflecting upon your overall evaluation are important skills not to be underestimated. They will help you to appraise and make critical judgements about psychological research and its application to the real world.

Skill builder activity

Questionnaire design

Transferable skill focus: problem solving

Key question: *What is wrong with this scale?*

To what extent do you agree with the statement: 'Statistics is my life'?

Totally agree	Very strongly agree	Strongly agree	Agree	Most likely agree	Neutral	Most likely disagree	Disagree	Strongly disagree	Very strongly disagree	Totally disagree
1	2	3	4	5	6	7	8	9	10	11

Hint: Consider the scoring scale being employed.

You may think that this questionnaire is not unusual, but just consider what the researchers were trying to do. You have been asked to rate how much you agree with the given statement on the 11-point scale provided. At first glance, this may appear to be quite straightforward – indeed, you almost have an embarrassment of options from which to document your response.

This might be considered problematic. Try having a go at responding to the statement – do you find this easy or difficult? Why? Try reducing the size of the scale to three points. What problems might this then entail in responding?

Skill builder review

The original 11-point scale is so large that arguably there are little meaningful gradations or differences between each successive category on the scale (for example, is there really a difference between 'very strongly disagree' and 'totally disagree'?) You might find that research participants cannot distinguish between these and so they may respond apathetically. Second, while the inflation of a scale is useful if you wish to conduct a parametric analysis, inflating to such an artificial extent as 11 points may result in data that does not reflect any genuine psychological distinction. Conversely, should the scale be too small (for example, 'totally agree' versus 'neutral' versus 'totally disagree'), you may find your questionnaire fails to capture the richness and complexity of the construct. Furthermore, your participants may feel shoehorned into giving a response that is not truly representative of how they feel.

This activity helps develop your problem-solving skills. This skill is of crucial importance in both academic and research matters. The activity encourages you to think through the issues and possible problems associated with the design of a questionnaire scale – a common task in psychology degrees!

Assignments

1. We have examined the different levels of measurement in the quantification of data. It is important to realise that these levels of measurement are also used in the assigning of individuals into different experimental groups. What levels of measurement does each of these following groups represent? Consider what the dangers are of being bound within a specified level of measurement. What (if any) assumptions are being made?

   a. Males and females

   b. Psychotic and non-psychotic

   c. Participants have the speed at which they respond on a reaction-timed task measured across a temperature range of −7°C to +5°C at 1°C intervals. This is to measure the effect of temperature upon motor performance.

2. Consider the debate between ordinal and interval measures. Do these differences seem to be academic and trifling in terms of research in the real world, or might they have profound implications? If so, what are they?

3. Is a systematic error worse than a random error? Imagine you have conducted a research project investigating the effects of a new drug treatment for symptoms of multiple sclerosis.

When you begin analysing the data, you quickly realise there is a systematic error in your measurements. Is this catastrophic? What could you do? Would the situation be any different if you uncovered a random error?

Summary: what you have learned

This chapter has introduced you to issues surrounding the measuring of data. You should now be aware of the different levels of measurement, how these can be distinguished from each other and the implications thereof. In addition, the discrete/continuous nature of data variables has been presented.

You should have an appreciation of the critiques levied at data measurement, how assigning numerical values to concepts may artificially constrain or fail to capture the richness of data or experiences and views of participants. The issue of erroneous measurement and its implications were discussed, and you were quizzed on how researchers might try to avoid or minimise these.

By reading this chapter and completing the exercises contained within, you are on your way to developing your critical and creative thinking skills. Additionally, the tasks set will have tested your problem-solving abilities. These qualities are essential for anyone studying psychology as you are expected to be able to competently dissect and understand the finer points of research measures.

Further reading

Dancey, C and Reidy, J (2011) *Statistics without Maths for Psychology*. Harlow: Prentice Hall.

Interested readers (or if you have to study statistics!) should consult this book to help with any statistical issues to which we have referred. Statistics can feel like an impenetrable subject at the best of times, but this book manages to strip away the scary equations and formula in order to get to grips with how to conduct and interpret statistics. Highly recommended.

Jamieson, S (2004) Likert scales: how to (ab)use them. *Medical Education*, 38(12), 1365–2923.

Some people have a tendency to treat ordinal data as though they were intervals in order to conduct more sophisticated statistical analyses. This is controversial. Others argue that, statistically speaking, ordinal measures usually conform to the **central limit theorem** *(basically, this means so long as you have a large enough number of participants in your study, the properties of this data will be approximate to that of a normally distributed dataset). Due to this phenomenon, some suggest that it is therefore permissible to treat and analyse ordinal measures as though they were of interval level. If you wish to learn more about this debate, we suggest you read this straightforward account.*

Rubia, K, Smith, A and Taylor, E (2007) Performance of Children with Attention Deficit Hyperactivity Disorder (ADHD) on a Test Battery of Impulsiveness. *Child Neuropsychology*, 13(3), 276–304.

This readable paper gives an account of a selection of different tasks used to measure levels of impulsivity.

Velleman, PF and Wilkinson, L (1993) Nominal, Ordinal, Interval, and Ratio Typologies Are Misleading. *The American Statistician*, 47(1), 65–72.

A critique of Stevens' four levels of measurement.

Chapter 4

Experimental designs

Learning outcomes

The purpose of this chapter is to introduce you to the bedrock of scientific research – the experiment. We will discuss the various aspects involved in designing and conducting an experiment, helping you to design your own experiments and critically appraise those carried out by others.

By the end of this chapter you should:

- *be able to identify the types of variables used in research investigations;*
- *comprehend the different formats used in experimental designs;*
- *appreciate the importance of randomly allocating your participants;*
- *understand the pros and cons of experimental designs;*
- *be aware of issues relating to the setting in which research is carried out;*
- *have developed your organisational skills;*
- *have practised your problem-solving skills.*

Introduction

Conducting research is a fundamental step in improving knowledge of any given topic. We construct theories about how things work and how factors and constructs relate to each other in order to understand the underlying mechanisms and processes. We then conduct strictly controlled experiments in order that we may consolidate, refine or repudiate these theories that inform our understanding. In short, conducting research experiments is the first step to learning.

So what is an experiment?

Designing an experiment allows us to learn the finer points about cause and effect. That is, when conducting an experiment, we are primarily interested in the effect that one variable may have on some behaviour – the effect on this behaviour being measured by a second variable. A variable itself is simply the property of some event, object or person that may have different values at different times depending on whatever experimental conditions have been determined. It is examining the effect of these different conditions that is of interest to a researcher. By systematically controlling or manipulating a variable of interest, we can see if this has any demonstrable and thus a measurable effect on another variable. In contrast, if we were to adopt a passive role in research and not instigate any changes to our variables, we can only observe participants' behaviour and thus are limited in making any inferences regarding cause and effect (also see Chapter 6, pages 86–7, on correlational designs).

For example, let us consider the relationship between the consumption of sugary sweets and oral hygiene in young children. We could, in theory, give varying amounts of sweets to different groups of children (say 0g and 100g per day) over the course of one month, and then record the number of fillings they have at the end of this time period. What would be of interest in this experiment is to demonstrate that it was varying the amount of sugary sweets eaten that caused varying levels of poor oral hygiene. Nothing else had varied, and so it would be possible to infer that the high daily intake of sweets caused high levels of fillings in children, and that the lower daily intake of sweets caused fewer fillings to be required. We can see here in our experiment how the levels in one variable (sweets) are said to **co-vary** with the recorded levels of another variable (number of fillings).

Types of variables

You have, no doubt, just realised from the above experiment that different types of variables must exist. This is true – in fact, there are four main types of variables involved in experiments with which you need to familiarise yourself.

1. Independent variable (IV).

2. Dependent variable (DV).

3. Confounding variable.

4. Extraneous variable.

The independent variable is of most interest to a researcher. This is the variable that is systematically manipulated within an experiment (independently of changes to any other variable) in order to determine the effect this manipulation may have on a particular behaviour, skill or response. This deliberate variation means that the IV itself must therefore be composed of discrete levels, i.e. that different amounts or levels of the IV will be given in the experiment. In the previous example, the IV would have been the sugared sweets given to the participants – the manipulation gave us two levels of the IV to study (i.e. whether they received 0g or 100g of sweets per day). These two levels are generally referred to as the control and experimental conditions. The control condition is included to act as a baseline measure – as these children received no amount of the IV (i.e. 0g of sweets per day). In contrast, children in the experimental condition did receive a pre-specified level of the IV (100g of sweets per day).

This manipulation of the IV is the fundamental basis of any research experiment. If the number of fillings is found to co-vary with the levels of sweets consumed on a consistent basis, then this experiment will permit a **causal inference** that it was the IV that caused the changes to the scores, i.e. that it was the high levels of sweets consumed on a daily basis that caused poor oral hygiene in this group of children. Rather than choosing two seemingly arbitrary levels of the IV (0g and 100g of sweets), we may wish to examine the cause-and-effect relationship more closely by **parametric modulation** of the IV so that we have a systematic range of levels instead – for example, 0g, 25g, 50g, 75g and 100g (see Figure 4.1 for a representation of this). Here we have demonstrated that the number of fillings required co-varies with the levels of the IV in a consistent manner.

Figure 4.1: *Results from the sugary sweets experiment (parametric modulation of IV)*

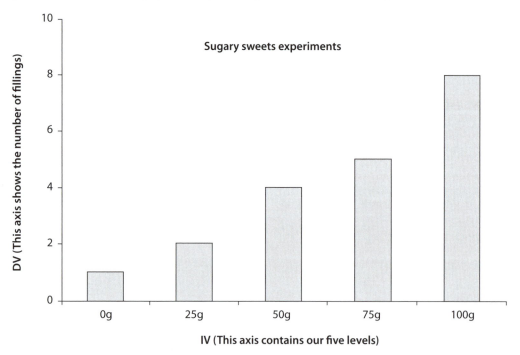

Task — How do we know how much to manipulate the IV? What do you think a researcher may use as a guide to what may be the most appropriate quantities by which to vary the levels of the IV?

In contrast, the dependent variable is the behaviour or response that is being measured and recorded by the researcher in order to assess if there is an effect of manipulating the IV. The amount that the scores on the DV will vary by is dependent upon the variations in the IV (number of sweets). In relation to our experiment, the DV is poor oral hygiene – specifically the number of fillings required at the end of the experiment by our two groups of children (0g of sweets and 100g of sweets).

As you can imagine, dependent variables themselves are not homogeneous – they can be wildly different in terms of what is being measured in the experiment. For example, researchers investigating children with dyslexia will employ DV(s) that are very different from other researchers who may wish to interview people in order to gain their perspectives on some topical debate. It is even possible to use multiple DVs in order to provide a diverse and informative set of measures within the same experiment – for example, we may wish to measure the effect that physical exercise may have on our health; this may mean we need to record the heart rate, blood pressure, weight, fat levels, blood oxygen levels, lung capacity and recovery time in our participants. Each of these dependent variables confers a unique and edifying contribution to our understanding of the impact that physical exercise can have on health. Each of these separate DVs possesses different properties that can be delineated according to an increasing level of complexity (Stevens, 1946). Principally these include:

- nominal;

- ordinal;

- interval;

- ratio.

See Chapter 3 (pages 36–9) for a more detailed explanation of the different types of dependent variables.

A confounding variable is quite an unpleasant thing to have in your research study, and care must be made when first designing the experiment to minimise the likelihood of this making an appearance. A confounding variable is an entity that changes simultaneously with the manipulation of the IV in an experiment. The result of this situation is (annoyingly) an inability to conclude that the pattern of results obtained in the data is due to your deliberate manipulation of the IV – it could quite plausibly be due to this previously 'hidden' third variable.

To illustrate, let us revisit the earliest incarnation of the experiment we constructed that measured the effects of consuming sugary sweets and the number of fillings in young children. Any difference in the number of fillings (the DV) between our two groups (the two levels of our IV: those who received 0g and 100g of sweets per day) may be caused by this direct manipulation. However, what if we later found out that those participants in the control group (0g per day) brushed their teeth twice a day, but those in the experimental group (100g per day) did not brush their teeth at all? This has a serious effect on the validity of our earlier conclusion. The fact that the experimental group needed more fillings may not be due to the fact they ate sugary sweets (as we proposed based on the design and subsequent results of our experiment), but may be due to the fact that they did not brush their teeth. Both the sugar levels and brushing of teeth co-vary with the number of fillings required, and we have no way to disentangle them.

Our study is now confounded by this teeth-brushing variable and is thus seriously undermined. We may prefer our interpretation of the results, but the new alternative account explains the pattern of results just as well. This is a poor state of affairs; an experiment with two possible explanations of the outcome is worthless. As we failed to control for this hidden variable (brushing of teeth), our experiment is now invalid – we'll be laughed at in conferences, it won't get published in a journal and we will fail to get acclaim from our colleagues! In short, it is better to be proactive than reactive – meticulous planning at the design stage would have helped identify this confound and so we could have controlled for it, and thus avoided having to dispute the validity of our own results.

Task — If you were designing this sugary snacks experiment, how might you control for the frequency of brushing teeth in your participants? Can you identify any other potential confounds?

Similarly, **extraneous variables** are also considered to be undesirable elements in a research study. The variables themselves are of no direct interest to the researcher yet could interfere or exert some deleterious effect on the outcome of the experiment. These are generally portrayed to be nuisance variables, though do not be swayed by this characterisation: this may be under-estimating their potential to upset an experiment. Examples may include the time of day when testing your participants, their mood or level of motivation – each of these instances may not have any direct bearing on the interests of the researcher conducting the experiment, but if consistently found to be present may exert a confounding effect on the pattern of results. For example, a recent study by Danner and Phillips (2008) investigated the well-known phenomenon of teenagers being unable to perform optimally early in the morning. By delaying the start time of school by an hour, they recorded a 16.5 per cent drop in teenage car accidents compared to a 7.8 per cent increase in other schools. While this may not be of interest to a research experiment that investigates the developmental trajectory of linguistic capability across the lifespan, if the researcher just happens to test teenage volunteers exclusively in the morning and other age groups later in the day, this extraneous variable suddenly steps up from being a mere nuisance to confounding the entire experiment! Repeat the mantra: care and attention to detail is needed when planning the design of experiments.

Table 4.1: *Illustrating key variables*

Key types of variable	Explanation
Independent (IV)	This is the variable that you, as a researcher, wish to manipulate, or systematically alter, in order to study its effects. *For example, levels of a drug, exercise, patient health groups, memory training etc.*
Dependent (DV)	The DV is used to assess the effects of altering the independent variable(s). Put simply, it is the thing being measured in an experiment! *For example, heart rate, intelligence, size of child's vocabulary, personality traits, EEG waveforms etc. See Chapter 3 for more details.*
Confounding	Nasty things! These variables happen to change simultaneously when the independent variable is altered – thus you don't know if results in your experiment are due to the intended manipulation of your IV, or the presence of some third variable. *For example, one experiment investigated the link between contact sports and subsequent mild brain injury. Their results demonstrated that ex-footballers performed worse than ex-swimmers on tests of cognitive functioning. However, footballers traditionally consume more alcohol, which is known to impair performance on such tests.*
Extraneous	These variables are not of inherent interest to your experiment, but could still potentially affect it. *For example, you are interested in linguistic development, and so conduct an experiment that investigates the reading skills of children of different ages. Might the socioeconomic status of the children's parents affect their scores?*

Experimental design

So far we have outlined the basic principles and variables that are required in an experiment. The questions probably on your lips are, 'How do you go about creating an experiment? How do you decide what to do with your participants? What should be manipulated?' Well, first things first, you need to design your experiment so that you can exert tight control over what happens in it. Let's revisit our experiment on sugary sweets. We wanted to investigate the effect of giving varying levels of sweets to children on their oral hygiene. This is the IV and DV respectively. Now we need to decide what to do with potential participants recruited to the study. We need to assign them to the different experimental conditions in our study, and wouldn't you know it, there are different forms that our experiment can take. The two basic designs are:

- between-participants
- within-participants.

In a **between-participants** design (sometimes referred to as between-subjects, between-groups or an independent measures), essentially we split up our participants into different groups. Each group will then be assigned to a different condition as determined by the number of levels in the IV being manipulated. Table 4.2a depicts this process: participants 1–10 are assigned to group 1 and are in the control condition (0g of sweets per day), whereas participants 11–20 are assigned to group 2 and are in the experimental condition (100g of sweets per day). Both groups will then be measured on the same DV (the number of fillings required at the end of one month) and have these scores compared in a statistical analysis to see if any difference is significant. One advantage of this design is that should participants withdraw from the study (**attrition**) or be hard to recruit, unequal sample sizes can be tolerated and data still analysed.

In contrast, in a **within-participants** design (also known as within-subjects or **repeated-measures**), the participants are not split up into groups. Instead, they are kept as 'one' group and are tested repeatedly in all of the conditions that exist in the experiment. While this may initially sound confusing, in practice it is very straightforward. In Table 4b, you can see that our participants will be in the control condition, but then will also do the experiment again, but this time be in the experimental condition. Each participant's score in one condition is then compared with their own score in the other condition, and these differences within the group are analysed for statistical significance. As each participant is tested twice, this effectively means each participant acts as their own control, and thus serves to remove any natural differences in performance as measured on

Table 4.2: *Allocation of people into experiments using either: a) between-participants and b) within-participants designs*

4.2a

Control condition (0g of sweets) Group 1	Experimental condition (100g sweets) Group 2
Participant 1	Participant 11
Participant 2	Participant 12
Participant 3	Participant 13
Participant 4	Participant 14
Participant 5	Participant 15
Participant 6	Participant 16
Participant 7	Participant 17
Participant 8	Participant 18
Participant 9	Participant 19
Participant 10	Participant 20

4.2b

Control condition (0g of sweets) Condition 1	Experimental condition (100g sweets) Condition 2
Participant 1	Participant 1
Participant 2	Participant 2
Participant 3	Participant 3
Participant 4	Participant 4
Participant 5	Participant 5
Participant 6	Participant 6
Participant 7	Participant 7
Participant 8	Participant 8
Participant 9	Participant 9
Participant 10	Participant 10

the DV that may exist when comparing different groups of participants. However, attrition is of particular concern: should any participant wish to leave before completing all the conditions in the study, they unbalance it and so will have to have all their data removed from the analysis.

Occasionally, research studies are conducted in which it is simply not possible to manipulate the IV of interest, thus preventing the random allocation of participants into groups. These are known as quasi-experiments (meaning 'not really' or 'almost'). Do not consider these to be inferior studies: on occasion it simply is not possible to manipulate the IV.

Task — An example of the above is sex – if we are interested in the differences between men and women, then obviously we cannot randomly allocate people into either of these groups; they are already male or female. Instead, participants are 'pre-assigned' to such groups on the basis of some inherent characteristic they possess – for example, children versus adults; diabetics versus healthy controls. Can you think of any more examples?

Participants

One very important factor we have conveniently sidestepped so far concerns the participants in a research study. In an experiment with a between-participants design, we will be testing the driving ability performance of two groups (caffeine versus **placebo**). Our experiment has been carefully designed so that (hopefully) we may infer that any difference in performance between our two groups is because of our deliberate experimental manipulation. In order to comply with this, we must first assume that our two groups of participants are equal in terms of their performance. If we stop people in the street at random and test their driving ability, we will find that there are people who are better at driving than others; their natural ability to drive is very good regardless of what group they may be allocated. However, we need to avoid one group having better drivers than the other – otherwise this may confound the experiment and any difference we see may not be attributable to our caffeine versus placebo pill-popping. Not only must we randomly sample participants from the general population when first recruiting (see Chapter 1, page 5), but we must also randomly allocate them to our groups in order to balance natural driving ability across both groups. In this way, we are likely to have an even variety of good, bad and fair drivers in each group; this means when we do our analysis, the amount that the 'natural driving ability' scores vary between our two groups is relatively small, and so if we do see any difference in scores after treatment, we can be more confident these differences are because of our experimental manipulation – caffeine versus placebo.

Task — Why don't we simply test the two groups before we start with any type of manipulation, treatment or intervention to make sure the two groups are equal?

So how do we randomly allocate people to our groups? This is contentious, and harder to achieve satisfactorily than you may think. Sorting people alphabetically by their surname is not advisable – you may find that certain names are more common (for example, Smith) and so introduce a bias in numbers. Sorting people according to the order they first contacted you about participating is not recommended either – you may find your first lot of participants are quite eager and keen to take part, but the latter half less so, and this may affect your groups (this is particularly true of psychology students who need to collect credits). A variant on this might be to alternate the weeks of recruitment – one week is for the control group, the next the experimental group. Again, this is fraught with potential bias – it lacks any real semblance of randomness. Some researchers may (literally) flip a coin each time they first meet a participant for testing – odds are that over the course of enough flips they should have an equal number of participants randomly allocated to each group. Others may prefer to draw up some sort of spreadsheet with a pre-allocated code next to the number and alternate on that basis.

If we decide to use a within-participants design instead and only have one group, you still shouldn't rest on your laurels as there is a separate batch of issues to concern you! When using a between-participants design, as our groups only experience one treatment condition we effectively test our groups at the same time. In a within-participants design, they experience multiple conditions. An immediate problem is the order in which we present these conditions. If we use the same fixed order of conditions, this will introduce a confounding variable to the experiment. For example, if we studied the effects of 0mg, 10mg, 20mg and 30mg of caffeine on driving ability in that order and note that skills improve – we might conclude that they are better due to the increased caffeine levels making them more alert and responsive. However, might we also be witnessing a **carry-over effect**? Skills learned in one trial are transported to subsequent trials. Could it be that people are getting better at driving simply because they are getting practice at it? Conversely, people could get bored or fatigued and have a drop in performance instead.

One solution is to randomise the order in which the participants experience the different conditions within an experiment. If we control the order of conditions to be presented, then in effect we will negate the likelihood of these carry-over effects. Again, we may flip a coin to decide the order of events for each participant, or employ more complicated methods to **counterbalance** studies with numerous conditions. For example, if we had a study with three conditions – A, B and C – then in order to present these randomly to our participants we would need six configurations: some would be tested in the order of ABC, while others would be ACB, BAC, BCA, CAB or CBA. However, these **complete counterbalanced** designs are exhaustive! A study with four conditions (A, B, C and D) would require 24 presentation orders; five conditions would require 120. A more resourceful technique is **partial counterbalancing**, such as the balanced **Latin-squares design**.

In Table 4.3 we have four conditions (A, B, C and D) within a 4 x 4 grid, which details the set order of the four conditions to be presented in four separate sequences (participants are assigned to these sequences). In this grid, we vary the order of conditions both along the rows and columns

Table 4.3: The balanced Latin-squares design

Sequence order number	Presented order of conditions within experiments			
	1st trial	2nd trial	3rd trial	4th trial
1	A	B	C	D
2	B	D	A	C
3	C	A	D	B
4	D	C	B	A

by virtue of mirror-reversing them. Consequently, the order of conditions experienced by participants in sequences 1 and 4 are reversed (ABCD versus DCBA), and the same applies to participants in sequences 2 and 3 (BDAC versus CADB). Furthermore, the order of conditions in the first trial is in reverse to that of the fourth trial (ABCD versus DCBA), as is the second and the third (BDAC versus CADB). The efficiency of this design requires only four orders of presentation – not the 24 that would otherwise be required.

An interesting middle ground between the within and between participant designs is the use of **matched pairs**. In this method, rather than randomly assigning participants to different groups, the researcher tries to match up each participant in one group with a participant in the other group. These matches can be made on a variety of measures, but depending on the nature of the experiment typical examples might include age, sex, IQ, weight and socioeconomic status. As participants are as closely matched as possible on these measures, the natural variance in ability between the groups is (arguably) reduced. Some researchers therefore advocate that it is now permissible to treat this as a within-participants design and so use this particular family of statistics. This step is controversial, namely because this purported reduction of variance in natural ability between the groups can be disputed. Switching from a between-participants to a within-participants analysis would mean that you are more likely to find a statistically significant difference in scores, or conversely are more likely to make a **type I error** and think you have found a statistical difference when in actual fact this does not truly exist (as opposed to a **type II error** in which you think you do not have a significant finding when in fact you do).

Researcher and participant bias

While we can randomly assign participants to groups or the order of conditions, there are further problems relating to our participants and the researcher. Suppose that the researcher has allocated participants into groups and now begins the treatments and testing – an obvious problem here is that the researcher knows who is in which group; this may bias the results being collected. Unwittingly, the researcher may communicate assertions or expected patterns of results that in some way may affect the relationship with the participants and ultimately affect the participants' performance on whatever measures are being collected. Similarly, the participants may exhibit demand characteristics and behave differently – they may (again, unwittingly or not) try to behave or perform according to how they think the researcher wants them to (or, indeed, in the opposite direction). An illustration of this confounding variable is the **nocebo effect** – if you tell participants in a study that there are unpleasant side effects associated with a drug that is being studied (for example, headaches or flushes), then they may experience them – even if they received the dummy placebo. This is why many experiments will employ a design that is **double-blind**, i.e. neither the researcher nor the participants are aware of what group or condition they are in and so this will reduce a potential source of bias and improve the validity of the results.

Task —
At the Hawthorne works in Chicago during the early twentieth century, a series of studies revealed that the productivity levels of workers rose when changes to the workplace were first instigated. However, they soon returned to their original levels over time. It transpired that when members of staff were aware that they were being overtly monitored, they upped their work rate accordingly. How do you think this might affect participants in research?

Even if we employ a double-blind design, is it possible for participants/researchers to find out what condition they are in? Years ago I took part in a brain-imaging study that used ketamine to simulate the symptoms of psychosis; the study employed a within-participants design and was double-blind. However, during the first trial I did not experience anything unusual and so knew that I was given a placebo; the second trial, however, was much more . . . interesting! Can you think of other situations in which the condition may be revealed inadvertently?

Other experimental designs

There are other types of experimental designs, and variations on the two basic designs we have presented. In no particular order, these include the mixed-design, pre- and post-test design, single-case studies, time course-based (see Chapter 5), and finally (though, strictly speaking, it is not experimental) there is the correlational design (see Chapter 6).

So far we have only illustrated experiments that manipulate one independent variable. However, it is possible to manipulate two or more IVs simultaneously while still using between- and within-participant designs. It is also possible to employ a **mixed factorial design**, which is simply a

Table 4.4: *Allocation of participants in a mixed 2*(2) experimental design*

IV_2 – pills	IV_1 – drink	
	Water (Group 1)	Alcohol (Group 2)
Placebo	Participant 1	Participant 6
	Participant 2	Participant 7
	Participant 3	Participant 8
	Participant 4	Participant 9
	Participant 5	Participant 10
Caffeine	Participant 1	Participant 6
	Participant 2	Participant 7
	Participant 3	Participant 8
	Participant 4	Participant 9
	Participant 5	Participant 10

combination of both the between and within approaches. This therefore requires that at least two IVs are manipulated. As an example, we may wish to design a study that assesses the effects of drinking (IV_1) and pills (IV_2) on driving ability (DV).

As can be seen in Table 4.4 above, we have a 2*(2) mixed experimental design. IV_1 is the between-participants variable – it has two levels (water versus alcohol) and therefore we will need two groups of participants (1–5 and 6–10 respectively) who will be subjected to experience either level. However, IV_2 is a within-participants variable (as denoted by the pair of brackets), which also has two levels: placebo versus caffeine. This means both of our water and alcohol groups will be tested twice, i.e. they will experience both the placebo and caffeine levels during the experiment. If we used a purely 2*2 between-participants design, then we would need four groups of different people. For a (2*2) within-participants design, then one group would need to be tested in all four conditions in total.

This may seem a complicated design (and we have only presented two variables each with two levels here: it is possible to have many more in an experiment), but all this represents is the basis for more intricate experiments. Rather than being hamstrung by only testing one variable at a time, or being forced to use multiple groups or even confined to one group of participants, here you get the best of both worlds. It is employed by researchers when it is the most sensible and pragmatic approach to conducting an investigation, most commonly when the planned experiment will contain a large number of conditions. For example, let's imagine we wish to investigate an experiment with a 2*4 design. This means we have two IVs, one with two levels and the second with four levels; thus, overall we have eight conditions. If we deployed a between-participants design, then we would need to recruit eight groups of people; if we decided on a (2*4) within-participants design, then we would require our recruits to sit through eight lots of testing. By using a 2*(4) mixed-design approach, we would need two groups of people to be tested four times (or the converse – it all depends on which IV is going to be the between-participants factor).

A variant of this design is the pre- and post-test design. Imagine that you have designed an experiment to assess the effectiveness of a new psychological treatment for depression; you have managed to recruit two groups of participants with clinical depression, one of which will be the experimental group (they receive the new treatment) while the other will be the control group (they remain on the waiting list). The experiment itself is composed of three phases.

1. Administer the Beck Depression Inventory (BDI) prior to any intervention.

2. Give treatment/waiting list.

3. Administer BDI again post-intervention.

Here we have two IVs: intervention (treatment versus waiting list) and time (pre- versus post-BDI scores). While we can analyse these two factors simultaneously and look at how time (pre- versus post-) and group (control versus experimental) may have affected the depression scores, or even use the pre-intervention scores as a co-variate when analysing the post-treatment scores, quite often researchers use a far simpler and more intuitive analysis. Instead, they subtract the pre- from the post-intervention scores for each individual participant and then analyse these differences between the two groups. In relation to the graph in Figure 4.2, essentially we would be deleting one dark-shaded column from the other, and the same again for the light-shaded column – the size of what is left behind is an indicator of how well the intervention has worked: if the remaining bar is small, then there has been a corresponding small impact of the intervention; in contrast, a large residual indicates that it has evinced a relatively large effect on the depression scores.

However, there are issues with this design. The very fact we have given participants the pre-intervention test may have inadvertently affected their scores – for example, reading the items on the depression questionnaire may have alerted them to symptoms they were previously unaware of and thus inflated their scores. Thus, we would need to include another two groups who did not have this pre-intervention test (one of which will receive the treatment while the other goes on the waiting list) and then compare post-intervention test scores. This is a **Solomon four-group design**, and adds an expensive layer of complexity to a previously elegant design. Another critique is one of ethical concerns – in this example, although we are assessing the effectiveness of this new psychological therapy for depression, is it right to deny patients on the waiting list a chance of treatment?

Figure 4.2: Hypothesised scores in a pre- and post-intervention study on treatment of depression

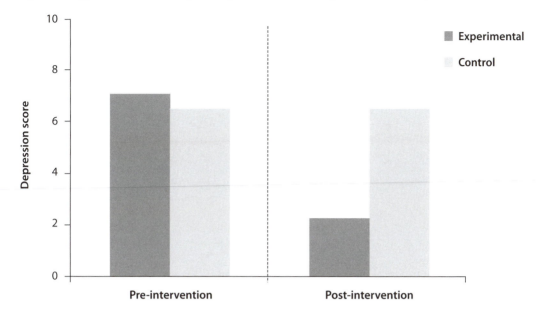

Another approach that has seen widespread use in psychology is the use of the **case study** or **single-subject** experimental design. Previously, we have conducted experiments that involve groups of participants, but here we are studying one participant. Quite often this will involve a diverse range of in-depth assessments that are repetitive in nature – single case studies are tested under both the experimental treatment and control conditions (using an AB format, or multiples thereof as in Figure 4.3) and scores from each condition can then be compared to elucidate cause and effect.

Due to this in-depth testing, researchers can elicit a wealth of detailed data that is simply not possible across numerous participants. Quite often in psychology, case studies are patients with striking characteristics that are so rare that getting enough participants together to form a group is nigh-on impossible – for example, those with an acute injury to a specific part of the brain, people with a particular genetic disorder or a victim who survived an assault. These case studies can illuminate or help develop theories underpinning the topic at hand. A great example is HM. He had intractable epilepsy, which in 1953 was cured by surgically removing both medial temporal lobes. As a result, he suffered anterograde amnesia and was unable to form long-term memories from that point onwards. The investigations and publications about HM provided a truly enormous leap forward in the understanding of memory formation.

However, the very strengths of a single-subject case design have arguably highlighted its weaknesses. As a unique individual is being studied, how confident can we be as to the level of both internal and external validity? Can we be confident of the cause-and-effect relationship if the experimental conditions cannot be randomly presented (surely order and carry-over effects must be

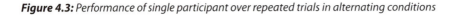

Figure 4.3: *Performance of single participant over repeated trials in alternating conditions*

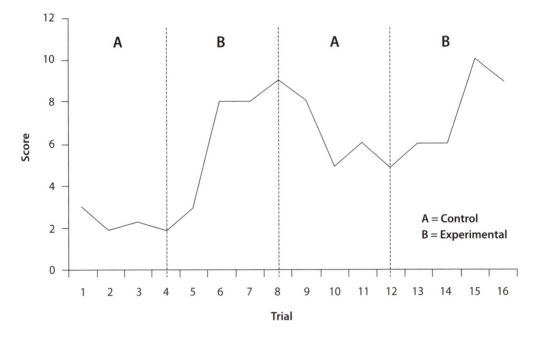

of concern?) Can we take the results and generalise these findings to others? The statistical analysis of single-subject case designs is another fraught matter – unless a control group of participants has also been tested, traditional statistical analyses cannot be performed, or else complicated (and questionable) ipsative analyses are reported. For a more informed debate on the use of case studies, we recommend that you read Robert Yin's excellent book on this subject (see Further reading).

Experimental settings

Now that you have been introduced to the types of experimental designs you can employ in research projects, we now turn our attention to the setting or context in which experiments can be conducted. Typically, these can be put into two categories: those conducted in **laboratory settings**, and those in **natural (or field) environments**.

Research studies that are conducted in a laboratory are what most people consider to be the prototypical example of an experiment. Participants are invited to take part in research studies and sequestered away from general settings. Quite often the study will take place in a specially constructed room or in testing booths that are soundproofed or have additional features depending on the nature of the investigation. This enables the researcher to control the immediate testing environment, and help eliminate extraneous variables. Typically, the participants are tested in isolation, free from distraction, and so arguably it is possible to gain a more reliable measure of their true ability.

In contrast, naturalistic experiments take place in real-world settings such as in people's homes, schools or other places that may be easily and frequently accessible. Due to this openness, the researcher cannot exert as much control over the immediate environment as they might be able to in a lab setting. However, this is to be balanced against the benefits of testing or observing people in a real-life setting – one that is not contrived. As a result, many people believe that 'field' experiments have high **ecological validity** and are more representative of how people are likely to behave or perform in real life rather than how they would behave in an artificial environment.

Task

We have presented the debate as here though the same type of experiment could be conducted in both types of environment. Generally speaking, however, it is the case that certain types of studies will be more suited to a particular environment. Look at this list of experiments and decide what might be the most appropriate setting and why.

- A test of short-term recall memory.

- Skin conductance recording while viewing images.

- Childhood interactions during pretend-play.

- Interpersonal dynamics in a political discussion.

- Completing personality questionnaires.

- Improving job-related performance.

Critical thinking activity

Design an experiment

Critical thinking focus: reflection

Key question: *What considerations do you need to make when designing a simple experiment?*

You are tasked with measuring the effect that caffeine has on improving reaction times. You are free to decide on your experimental design (between versus within) and the exact manipulation of your independent variable.

Consider the following questions to aid your reflection.

- What features will your experiment possess?

- How will you randomise the allocation of participants or the order of conditions presented?

- How will you control for the ingestion of caffeine?

- How will your participants be administered this?

- How exactly will you measure reaction time and avoid practice effects?

Critical thinking review

This activity helps develop your reflection skills in relation to designing and creating a psychological experiment. To assist you in this process, you were provided with a list of questions that helped you to consider some of the key features that need to be taken into account at the earliest stage of planning.

This is a fundamental step to ensure that the scientific rigour and validity of your experiment will stand up to review by your colleagues and peers. It is important to realise that no experiment can be perfect – there will always be factors that cannot be controlled sufficiently or taken into account. The next time you read a write-up of an experiment published in a journal article, try to provide a critique of the methodology. What weaknesses can you identify? Have the authors attempted to address these? How might you have improved on the design?

Skill builder activity

Confound it!

Transferable skill focus: problem-solving

Key question: *How can we avoid confounding variables?*

You wish to investigate the effect of a new cognitive-behavioural therapy on clinically diagnosed anxiety patients. You decide to have three conditions:

1. Waiting list control (i.e. no direct intervention).

2. Standard cognitive-behaviour therapy (the current therapeutic intervention).

3. Novel cognitive-behaviour therapy (the new-style therapeutic intervention).

You decide to implement a standard pre- and post-intervention test design. Initially, you will give each patient an anxiety questionnaire to obtain a baseline measure and their symptom severity. You will give the questionnaire again after completion of the ten-week course. You aim to recruit at least 60 patients via a GP practice that has agreed to advertise your study in its waiting room.

Having read the above proposal for an experiment, can you analyse its design in order to identify any potential confounding variables? What might you do to negate their effects?

Skill builder review

This proposed investigation of a new style of cognitive-behavioural therapy for anxiety may seem straightforward, but that could be its weakness. There are a variety of factors that you need to consider before commencing with this experiment. Think of the potential recruits – you are aiming to have 20 per group, but how will you randomly assign these? Anxiety levels can fluctuate depending on the specific type of disorder (for example, generalised anxiety disorder, obsessive compulsive disorder, a specific phobia) and in specific contexts. Will the patients have equally high levels of anxiety, or will some be moderately high and others severely so? Do you need to take into account whether the anxiety is acute or chronic? Is the anxiety reactive or not? As you are recruiting from a GP practice, might some patients be on prescribed medication? As you are only testing twice, might these snapshots be affected by external events? Would serial testing confer any advantage?

This activity helps develop your problem-solving skills in appraising and evaluating proposed research experiments. The ability to identify problems and improvise methods to avoid or negate such factors is of blistering importance in research. Failing to foresee and circumvent confounding variables will likely result in data that simply lacks any credible level of validity; the findings will be undermined and so cannot be used as a basis to increase knowledge of the subject area. In essence, you will have wasted your time, funding and energies.

Assignments

1. Fill in the gaps in Table 4.5, which provides a summary of the benefits and drawbacks of both between- and within-participant experimental designs. The key terms are provided underneath.

2. Consider the distinct advantages and disadvantages between studying a single participant versus numerous participants. At first glance, these two approaches would appear to be diametrically opposed, but is this necessarily true? Rather than reducing single-subject case studies to 'pilot study' status, should we instead portray them as a group with n=1 and treat them accordingly?

3. A common critique made of psychology is that it is not a hard science in the tradition of chemistry or physics. People are often portrayed as being dynamic, changeable and transient

Table 4.5: Pros and cons of the two basic experimental research designs

Design	Advantages	Disadvantages
Between-participants	Unequal sample sizes are _____ Participants kept _____ to study Carry-over effects are _____	_____ participants are required Financially _____ Differences might be due to _____ variation
Within-participants	_____ sample sizes required Participants act as their own_____ Financially _____	Participants' quitting is _____ Carry-over effects are _____ Aim of study may become _____

permissible	**identical**	**blind**	**negated**	**control**	**cheaper**	**more**
	expensive	**problematic**	**troublesome**	**individual**	**apparent**	

in their behaviour, opinions and performances. As such, can we really conduct experiments (in the traditional sense) on such an inconsistent sample? Does manipulating variables in a social-science experiment equate to that of a hard science experiment? Consider whether this critique is valid – are people really so unpredictable? Is social science any less valid?

Summary: what you have learned

An experiment is a research design in which an independent variable is actively changed or manipulated and scores on another variable (DV) are measured to determine whether fluctuations in the scores are dependent on our deliberate changes. In order to test the principle of cause and effect, there is a requirement to systematically vary the levels within an independent variable. Good planning during the design stage can help remove the likelihood of other variables confounding the experiment or at least making nuisances of themselves.

There are various forms that a research design can take, but essentially these are based on two methods: those that involve different groups of participants tested under different conditions, or those that involve one group of participants who are tested under all the conditions of an experiment. We discussed various methods of randomly allocating your participants to these different groups and conditions, and contrasted the settings in which types of research may be conducted.

Further reading

Danner, F and Phillips, B (2008) Adolescent Sleep, School Start Times and Teen Motor Vehicle Crashes. *Journal of Clinical Sleep Medicine*, 4(6), 533–535.

This paper reports on an investigation into the relationship between the time at which adolescents start school and car crashes. In the areas where schools had their teenage students start lessons later in the morning, they reported a corresponding 16.5 per cent drop in the number of reported car accidents.

Yin, RK (2009) *Case Study Research: Design and Methods*. 4th edition. London: Sage Publications.

The use of case studies is an innovative approach to conducting experimental research. This book is devoted to this topic and is a highly recommended read.

Chapter 5

Time course studies

Learning outcomes

This chapter outlines an experimental research design that we briefly mentioned in Chapter 4 – that of time course studies. This chapter will familiarise you with the concept of measuring changes over time – both intra- and inter-generational. Through the use of cross-sectional, longitudinal and sequential designs, it is possible to demonstrate changes in abilities and behaviours within the same individuals over time or across different age groups of participants. Perhaps not unsurprisingly, this type of research design is synonymous with the field of developmental psychology, in which we try to ascertain the trajectories of a diverse range of behaviours across the entire lifespan. What might surprise you, however, is that you have already learned much of the content contained within this chapter. . .

By the end of this chapter you should:

- *be able to differentiate longitudinal, cross-sectional and cross-sequential research designs;*

- *understand the advantages and disadvantages of each of these;*

- *be aware of issues relating to these designs;*

- *have developed your analytical and creative thinking skills;*

- *have practised your data skills.*

Introduction

In Chapter 4 we introduced the basic range of research designs that can be selected in order to conduct experimental investigations into the effects that manipulating independent variables may exert. This chapter will provide a focus on one variable that is often overlooked by students in research: the effect of time. These 'time course' studies measure the effect that age may have on any particular metric of interest. Rather than considering age to be a nuisance variable (or worse) and controlling for this among participants, the field of developmental psychology has this variable as a central tenet of its investigations – to research how behaviours, skills and attributes develop over the entire lifespan. Primarily, we will concentrate on measuring the effect of age expressed in three ways:

1. at an individual level (intra-generational) using the **longitudinal design**;

2. at a group level (inter-generational) using the **cross-sectional design**;

3. combining both of the above with sequential designs.

Longitudinal design

It is possible to study the effect that ageing or maturation may have within a single cohort, i.e. a group of people born at the same period of time. The basic premise behind this research is to follow this single cohort of participants and record their abilities at various time points in their lifespan. As an example of this longitudinal design, we may wish to study the stability of particular personality traits – for argument's sake, let's use agreeableness, openness and neuroticism. We could recruit a group of participants who were all 20 years old, and then test them at ten-year intervals until they are 70 years old. As you may have correctly surmised, this design is therefore akin to the within-participants (or repeated-measures) design of Chapter 4, in that the same participants are tested repeatedly on the same task over time. The manipulated variable in this example is age, as our participants will have their personality scores compared from across a variety of predetermined ages. (See Table 5.1 for an illustration of this design.)

Incidentally, there is a well-known television documentary series that makes use of this longitudinal design. First commissioned in 1964 with a programme called *7 Up*, as the eponymous title suggests every seven years a film crew interviews the same set of people to see how their lives (and views) have changed over the intervening years (see http://en.wikipedia.org/wiki/Up_Series for more details). The next entry in this series, *56 and Up*, is due to be screened in late 2011/12.

This was the original research design used in developmental psychology, and its benefits should be immediately apparent. By testing the same group of children on multiple occasions over a long period of time, it is possible to plot any changes in performance within the individual and tie this maturation of skill specifically to their ageing. We can then chart a true developmental trajectory due to *its capacity to take into account intraindividual variation* (Baltes, 1968, p147). This longitudinal approach enables us to collect data that is arguably more sensitive to age-related changes, but also will allow the analysis of such trends at the level of the individual. Indeed, while these

Table 5.1: *Example of a longitudinal research design*

Cohort (Year of birth)	Age at testing (years)					
1980	20	30	40	50	60	70
Year of testing	**2000**	**2010**	**2020**	**2030**	**2040**	**2050**

studies potentially can go on for a number of years, it is also possible to study a single cohort much more intensively over a shorter duration. This is known as the **microgenetic design**. This approach is quite often used by cognitive psychologists in their research in order to *illuminate the processes that are thought to promote developmental changes* (Schafer, 2009, p31). Quite simply, when children reach the age at which researchers think a particular developmental change is due to occur (for example, language skills, Gershkoff-Stowe and Smith, 1997), they are exposed to some experience such as an intervention designed to improve reading skills that may initiate this change. During this process, the children are tested repeatedly over a short timeframe (say, a few weeks) and their performances are monitored so as to chart any changes and development to this particular behaviour as it is occurring.

However, the longitudinal design suffers with the same problems as those already identified in the repeated-measures experimental design outlined in Chapter 4. You have, no doubt, considered that it can be an incredibly expensive and time-consuming process to collect data in a longitudinal study due to its repetitive nature, but also because of the enforced time period between data collection points. Indeed, our earlier personality study had ten-year gaps and lasted for 50 years in total. But related to this issue is attrition – the non-random loss of participants. People may simply wish to drop out of a study the longer and more involved it becomes; people may die, move away, or lose contact with the researchers. Indeed, of the original 14 children who participated in the *Seven Up* documentary, almost half either no longer participate or selectively drop in and out of the programmes. This selective drop-out then creates a further problem of selective survival. Can we class the participants who remain in the study in the same way as those who drop out? Might they be qualitatively different somehow? What is it that makes them decide to persevere and continue with the study? Could these factors influence the results? Longitudinal designs are already critiqued for poor internal validity – they are accused of failing to meet the criteria of representative sampling (as they use the same cohort), and the participants themselves have found to be of higher intelligence and socioeconomic status (read the article by Baltes (1968) for a detailed explanation of these critiques). Alternatively, the researchers themselves may change jobs, or lose interest in or funding for the study.

The longitudinal experimental design has an additional concern of confounding the personal history of the cohort with their effects of maturation. As longitudinal studies depend on the same cohort, if these participants happen to share some childhood experience (normative history influences), then any results stemming from this particular cohort might contain unexpected effects. To illustrate, let's set up a longitudinal study: you are interested in the political views of children as they develop from 10 years up to the age of 30. Your participants might all have experienced something in their youth that has somehow shaped them and their later behaviour or opinion. Examples might include being caught up in the London bombings of July 2007; having an older sibling or parent arrested during the recent student protests; or parents being made redundant due to the financial recession. It may be that these experiences (and not the normative maturation process) have affected and shaped your participants' latent political opinions. However, their experiences are not typical of others outside this particular cohort and so any conclusions you may draw from this longitudinal study may be erroneous and not representative. Thus the initial benefit of the longitudinal design in providing us with a glimpse of development within the individual can also be considered a drawback: these developmental changes may only be pertinent to a specific cohort.

Task — Consider the results of a study that was designed to investigate the development of social skills in a generation of children, which started in 1970 and finished in 2010. How relevant and applicable would you consider the results to be? What effects might the advent of children's TV, e-mail, social networking sites, texting and VOIP have on the opportunities afforded to people nowadays?

Cross-sectional design

A way to potentially avert the problems associated with following the same groups of participants over an extended period of time would be to compare groups of differently aged people on the same measure. This is known as a cross-sectional design; no doubt you will also have identified this as aping the between-participants design back in Chapter 4. The manipulated variable in such studies is age – this is what separates our groups. To use the previous personality experiment as an example, rather than start testing participants when they are 20 years old and retest them every ten years for the next half-century, we could effectively take a shortcut and test cohorts of different people aged 20, 30, 40, 50, 60 and 70 years old respectively (see Table 5.2 for an example of this design). Thus by employing a cross-sectional design, we could get all the testing done in a much shorter timeframe. This approach has the obvious benefit of making studies comparing the

Table 5.2: Example of a cross-sectional research design

Cohort (Year of birth)	Age at testing (years)
1930	70
1940	60
1950	50
1960	40
1970	30
1980	20
Year of testing	**2000**

development of abilities across the lifespan a much more feasible and achievable target for a research project.

However, it is important to point out that others (for example, Cook and Campbell, 1979) have argued that the cross-sectional design is, strictly speaking, not a true experimental design. Instead, they posit that this is merely a case of separate sample groups that are being tested. The age of participants is normally considered as a potentially confounding variable in between-groups designs, and thus is tightly controlled among the different groups; quite often researchers will go to great lengths to make sure that all their groups are of similar ages. However, in a cross-sectional design, this variable is suddenly thrust into the limelight and is itself the independent variable being examined.

The cross-sectional design is thus faced with all the critiques and problems that can be levied against the use of the between-participants approach. As an example, one drawback to cross-sectional designs is the assumption that the only difference between the cohort groups is their respective ages. In reality, there may be many variables along which the cohorts differ, but these differences we observe are presumed to be age related. These results may be confounded with other differences between the cohorts instead. For instance, if we compare people in their 20s, 30s, 40s, 50s, 60s and 70s on our personality measures, are we really obtaining a true reflection of age-related changes? Think of all the seismic changes that have happened over the intervening years: the end of the Second World War, the dour 1950s and the permissive 1960s, the financially restrictive 1970s and flamboyant 1980s, the birth of home computers and the internet in the 1990s and so on. Surely it is possible that it is these experiences that may have influenced the personality measures of each respective cohort and not simply their respective ages? If they do, then the study is confounded. It has been argued that, at best, *differences in cohorts can be described but the differences can not be definitively explained* (Woolf, 1998).

A more fundamental objection to this method of design is that we are no longer following the developmental trajectory at the level of the individual. By this, we mean it is no longer possible to demonstrate if or when changes occur in our participants as they are tested only once – cause and effect is implied rather than demonstrated. Additionally, rather than depicting the fluid development and gradual maturing of abilities within the individual as in longitudinal designs, the snapshots obtained from cross-sectional designs depict sudden, staccato changes in abilities across different age groups of different people. Plotting and inferring a developmental trajectory from data obtained with this design can be quite difficult; there may be widespread differences in performance between various age groups that are not age related, but rather are dependent on some other factor. The resulting trajectory may appear quite jerky and haphazard, and in some cases may even appear to be substantially different from data obtained with a longitudinal design. Take a look at the graphs in Figure 5.1 that demonstrate this.

Figures 5.1a and b: *Graphs of hypothetical data depicting age-related change in cognitive abilities obtained from a) cross-sectional and b) longitudinal research designs*

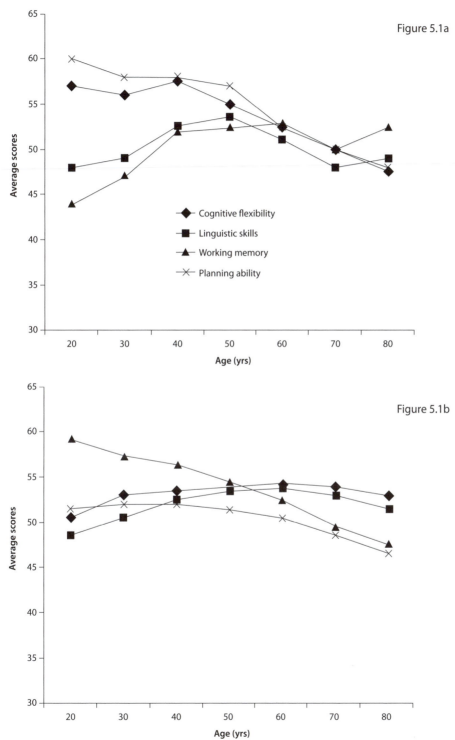

This figure displays the fictionalised developmental trajectories of cognitive abilities in participants across an age span from 20 to 80 years old. Figure 5.1a contains data collected with a cross-sectional design (with each cohort separated by ten years), while in Figure 5.1b the data was collected with a longitudinal approach. When comparing the two graphs visually, you may notice that the age-related trajectories of several cognitive skills appear to be different depending on the design used to obtain the data. The longitudinal study depicts these skills as an arc, each declining after the fifth decade. In contrast, the cross-sectional study has a more disjointed trajectory, with some of the skills apparently being resistant to age-related decline. For a depiction of actual data on the developmental trajectory of cognitive skills, you are encouraged to read a landmark paper by Schaie (1994) who, in his Seattle Study, collected data from thousands of participants and enabled the comparison from cross-sectional versus longitudinal-derived measures.

A third approach that is distinct from both longitudinal and cross-sectional approaches is the **time-lagged design**. As can be seen in Table 5.3, quite simply this entails measuring different cohorts of children at the same age; in this example, we would be comparing the performance of all participants when they were 20 years old (shaded).

Task — The purpose of the time-lagged design method is to investigate developments in performance that are associated with cultural changes. However, this approach is rarely used in psychology as it confounds two variables. Can you identify what these are?

Cross-sequential design

The **cross-sequential design** can be construed as an amalgamation of the previous two approaches. Essentially, it is a combination of both longitudinal (repeated-measures) and cross-

Table 5.3: Example of a time-lagged research design

Cohort (Year of birth)	Age at testing (years)					
1980	20	30	40	50	60	70
1990	10	20	30	40	50	60
2000	0	10	20	30	40	50
2010	X	0	10	20	30	40
2020	X	x	0	10	20	30
Year of testing	**2000**	**2010**	**2020**	**2030**	**2040**	**2050**

sectional (between-participants) designs, and might be viewed as somewhat similar to the mixed factorial designs outlined in Chapter 4 (see pages 58–9). The advantages behind both the longitudinal and cross-sectional designs are conferred upon sequential approaches, while the disadvantages associated with both are, arguably, somewhat attenuated.

As can be seen in Table 5.4, the cross-sequential design can facilitate the comparison of cohorts at many different time points, both longitudinally and across different age groups. By allowing the measurement of different cohorts (those born in 1980 to 2020) at different times (from 2000 to 2050), this approach will permit the researcher to examine genuine age (maturation) effects, but also those linked to cohort effects and the cross-generational influences precipitated by cultural or normative historical events. This is achieved because the cross-sequential design permits the simultaneous longitudinal testing of multiple cohort groups at different ages (left to right in table) while also enabling the testing of all available cohort groups at different cross-sections of age (top to bottom in the table). From the available contrasts, the cross-sequential approach can then facilitate the disentanglement of maturational from cohort effects and cultural events (if these sequential designs seem to be overly complicated, it should be borne in mind that these designs rely on even more complicated statistical analyses that, thankfully, are taught at postgraduate level).

Table 5.4: Example of permissible analyses of cohort data using the cross-sequential research design (shaded). We can now compare both longitudinal and cross-sectional data to eliminate biases stemming from cohort and cross-generational cultural events.

Cohort (Year of birth)	Age at testing (years)					
1980	20	30	40	50	60	70
1990	10	20	30	40	50	60
2000	0	10	20	30	40	50
2010	X	0	10	20	30	40
2020	X	X	0	10	20	30
Year of testing	**2000**	**2010**	**2020**	**2030**	**2040**	**2050**

Task — In Table 5.5 on page 76, half of the cells are missing their information. Using your knowledge of research designs, see if you can fill in these empty spaces using the row and column headers as a guide.

Table 5.5: *Main features of time series research designs*

Design	Number of groups	Advantage	Disadvantage	Equivalent to
Longitudinal	1		Effect of attrition is pronounced	
Cross-sectional		Quick to gather data cheaply		
Sequential	≥2	Can study change at both intra- and inter-generation level		Mixed factorial design

Critical thinking activity

The effects of age

Critical thinking focus: critical and creative thinking

Key question: *Is studying maturational effects with cohorts a valid research design?*

As was mentioned in the text, some researchers have critiqued the use of different aged cohorts as not being a true or valid research design. They argue that age is an insufficient variable from which to distinguish separate groups of participants. Furthermore, the assumption that differences observed between the cohorts in terms of performance are due to maturational effects is erroneous and invalid.

Consider the following questions to aid your critical appraisal.

– Do you agree with this viewpoint?

– What possible grounds might you have to reject this argument?

– Does this undermine decades of research in developmental psychology?

– How might the data from replicated studies provide a rebuttal?

Critical thinking review

This critical thinking activity will help consolidate your understanding of this chapter on time course studies. You were provided with a deeply critical viewpoint that was dismissive of a particular research design method. By having to argue against this one-sided statement, you were encouraged to formulate a reply that drew upon the content of this chapter and, no doubt, you succeeded. By articulating the answer in your own words, as opposed to simply restating what you have read like a parrot, you begin to understand the issues more intuitively and can help to improve the articulation and formulation of your answers.

Skill builder activity

Cross-sectional versus longitudinal design

Transferable skill focus: understanding and using data

Key question: How can research designs affect interpretation of data?

Take another look at the graphs in Figures 5.1a and b. These graphs depict the different developmental trajectories of a selection of skills across the lifespan. The hypothetical data was collected via cross-sectional and longitudinal designs; the figures depicted illustrate the developmental trajectory of both designs, and they seem to offer incongruent outcomes.

Using your knowledge of research designs, which graph do you think more accurately reflects the true picture of age-related decline in cognitive domains? Articulate your reasoning behind this decision.

Skill builder review

This activity shows the impact that research design may have on the understanding and interpretation of data. This is why time spent planning your research project and selecting the most appropriate experimental design is a key step in good research practice. Selecting a research design that is unsuitable for the study you wish to undertake can have dramatic effects on the outcome and interpretation of your results. If the research design is poorly conceived and inadequate, then it is unlikely that any complicated and intricate statistical analyses can remedy the situation. The true results may lie undetected.

This activity helps develop your understanding and use of data by bringing to your attention the issue of research designs. In the final year of your degree, you will need to design, implement and analyse a research project of your own. Not all research projects are similar; some topics and participant groups will require you to be flexible in how you deploy your research planning skills. The activity encouraged you to consider and articulate the reasons for choosing the most appropriate research design.

Assignments

1. You have just designed a study to investigate factors associated with the learning of a second language in school-aged children aged five to ten years old. You have decided to utilise a cross-sectional design and wish to recruit 70 children per year, giving you a total sample size of 700 participants. You approach several schools within your district. What do you envisage the day-to-day practicalities of attempting to complete such a study are? Should this approach not prove feasible, how might you adapt your project?

2. Participants withdrawing from a research study are an inevitable risk that any research will face. If you were planning on running a longitudinal study (in which attrition is particularly problematic), what might you do to try to minimise the likelihood of this occurring?

3. One of the biggest drawbacks to using longitudinal designs is the practice effects that may arise from using the same measures during the repeated testing phases. List the possible methods you could employ to undermine this critique.

Summary: what you have learned

This chapter on time course studies has built on your knowledge of experimental research designs from earlier chapters of this book. Hopefully, it has acquainted you with the variety of methods that are at your disposal in order to measure changes in behaviour (among others) over any period of time. The duration of this time can be both intra-generational (i.e. within the same people) and inter-generational (across different aged cohorts). We introduced you to a variety of designs: longitudinal, microgenetic, cross-sectional, time-lagged and sequential approaches, and gave a breakdown of the pros and cons associated with using each of these.

Further reading

Baltes, PB (1968) Longitudinal and Cross-Sectional Sequences in the Study of Age and Generation Effects. *Human Development*, 11(3), 145–171.

One of the first widespread texts on time-based research designs.

Cook, TD and Campbell, DT (1979) *Quasi-Experimentation: Design and Analysis for Field Settings*. Chicago, Illinois: Rand McNally.

Another classic text.

Schafer, DR (2009) *Social and Personality Development*. 6th edition. California: Wadsworth Publishing.

This is a general textbook on development, but contains a concise chapter on research methodologies.

Schaie, KW (1994) The course of adult intellectual development. *American Psychologist,* 49(4), 304–313.

This article is based on the author's epic and insanely immense study on the development of various cognitive skills and abilities during the adult lifespan. Known as the Seattle Study, over 5,000 participants were recruited to this project, which lasted for over 35 years. By employing a sequential design, it provided an opportunity to contrast findings from longitudinal and cross-sectional approaches to the study of cognitive decline. Recommended!

Woolf, LM (1998) *Theoretical Perspectives Relevant to Developmental Psychology*. Available online at http://www.webster.edu/~woolflm/perspectives.html [Last accessed 4 April 2011]

This website provides more details on the myriad of time-course-based research designs. It also has more information on the different subtypes of sequential designs. Useful if you are seeking an advanced level of knowledge.

http://en.wikipedia.org/wiki/Up_Series

Wikipedia provides a good overall account of the Up *television series. The lives and views of individual participants are discussed, along with how they developed over the intervening years. It's a shame that no video clips exist on this site (there is always YouTube!), but there is a DVD box set available.*

Chapter 6

Correlational designs

Learning outcomes

This chapter will outline another commonly used research design: correlation. This approach is typically used to assess the relationship, or the degree, of association between two or more variables. It is used extensively in research when manipulation of variables (as in a true experiment) is not possible; the reasons for this are outlined below. As such, this design method has been given a chapter of its own.

By the end of this chapter you should:

- *know why experimental manipulation of variables is not always possible;*
- *be able to convey a relationship between two variables as a correlation;*
- *demonstrate knowledge of the impact other variables may have on this relationship;*
- *be aware of the ability to predict future scores;*
- *have developed your critical and creative thinking skills;*
- *have practised your problem-solving skills.*

Introduction

In Chapter 4 you were introduced to the various forms of experimental designs that are commonly used in research. One example we tentatively included in this list was correlational designs, but this is not a true experimental design in its literal sense. As we explained previously, if we wish to make a causal inference between different variables (i.e. changes in one variable will effect changes in the second) we can demonstrate this in an experiment.

An experimental design allows us to tightly control and constrain what happens in a research study. We deliberately manipulate levels of the independent variable (IV) while holding everything else constant to ensure there are no confounding or extraneous variables that might interfere and confuse our findings. The result of our systematic alteration of the IV will then be demonstrated in proportional changes to our scores (the dependent variable: DV).

However, as we illustrated with a quasi-experiment, in certain situations it is not possible to manipulate the IV or randomly assign participants to different experimental conditions. Previously we used the classic example of sex – it simply is not possible to assign participants randomly to be in the male or female groups. In a study that is using a correlational design, we are faced with a similar restriction. Quite often we may wish to conduct research that, for various reasons, is not readily or ethically suitable for a true experimental analysis.

An illustration of this is needed. Let's say we wished to conduct a programme of research that investigated the speed of driving a car at impact and subsequent mortality rates. Our IV (the speed at which a car was travelling) would need to be parametrically manipulated to include the following conditions: 1mph, 10mph, 20mph, 30mph, 40mph, 50mph and so forth. We would then require our participants to drive a car at these speeds into a stationary object (for example, a brick wall) and then we would measure how many of them survive the impact.

As you can imagine, an ethics committee may have one or two reservations about approving such an experiment, and no doubt you may find it particularly difficult to recruit a sufficient number of participants to have reasonable confidence in the validity and reliability of your results. Instead, the experiment would have to rely on data from computer-simulated re-creations or from experiments involving crash test dummies. I would imagine the only way to involve data from people would be to obtain evidence from police investigations in which the impact was caught on camera (and thus speeds were calculated) and the casualties of each incident were known.

It may therefore be a better approach to turn such research on its head and instead ask a different question. Rather than attempt to demonstrate cause and effect, why not attempt to examine the **degree of association** between two variables?

Relationship between two variables

This is the central premise behind studies that utilise a correlational design. The researchers are measuring the relationship between two variables – their degree of association. Essentially, we wish to know if the changes in value on one variable might relate to changes in value on another variable.

For example, say we are interested in the height and weight of members from a local health club. We would need to measure each person's height and record it against their weight. We could then determine, as height increased, what the relationship to weight was. Similarly, we may wish to investigate the level of chocolate consumption in teenagers and plot this against the number of facial spots recorded. A correlational study can assess this relationship between two variables. If these two variables of interest are related to each other, then mathematically they are co-related. Their scores on both measures will co-vary. That term may sound like the beginning of a convoluted discussion on the vagaries of some statistical process, but all it means (essentially) is that as scores on one measure change (or 'vary'), the scores on the other measure will also vary.

Task —— Which of these pairs of variables do you think might correlate?

Hat size and intelligence	yes/no
Waist size and junk food consumption	yes/no
Mood and stress	yes/no
Personal wealth and shoe size	yes/no
Age and wisdom	yes/no
Number of wasp stings and happiness levels	yes/no
Degree of sunburn and time spent in agony	yes/no

Now what is especially useful about correlations is that these relationships can be summed up in an easily interpretable and intuitive number – the **correlation coefficient**.

The correlation coefficient

Without wishing to stray into the realm of statistics, the correlation coefficient is the end product of a calculation that probes the co-variance of these two variables (there is an excellent chapter on what exactly is calculated in a correlation in Dancey and Reidy, 2011; see Further reading, page 95). For our purposes, it is sufficient to say that this coefficient is simply a value that ranges between +1 and -1.

What can this correlation coefficient tell us? This coefficient has the advantage of simultaneously informing us of two key properties of a bivariate relationship, i.e. the association between two variables. It can determine:

- the direction
- the magnitude (strength).

Direction?

In the Task above you were presented with a list of paired variables and asked to consider if you thought they would be correlated. You will have noted that some of these pairs seem to have a straightforward relationship with each other (for example, waist size and amount of junk food eaten); others in an opposing manner (for example, number of wasp stings received and happiness levels), and some that do not appear to be related (for example, personal wealth and shoe size). These three outcomes reflect how it is possible to categorise the direction of a relationship between two variables: positive, negative or none.

We can use **scatterplots** to represent the relationship between variables. As can be seen in Figures 6.1a, b and c, we can plot each participant's scores on both variables (as denoted by a dot). Using these scatterplots, we may be able to tell the overall linear direction in which the dots are pointing, and thus whether they are positive, negative or have no relationship. Imagine if you were to draw a straight line through these dots that best represented this linear direction – this is exactly what the correlation coefficient is. It represents the line of best fit so that each dot is as close to the line as possible.

Positive relationships quite simply indicate that as scores on one variable increase, so do the scores on the second variable. As can be seen in Figure 6.1a, we have a scatterplot that represents the relationship between participants' height and weight measurements on the separate axes. If we look at the overall pattern of how the dots line up, it should be readily apparent that we can see an upward trend – the dots appear to go from the bottom left to the upper right of the scatterplot. This indicates that as height increases, so too does weight (or vice versa – we could swap the axes and still get the same relationship). Similarly, we may look at the dots in reverse – as height decreases, so too does weight. Any correlation coefficient that is positive (i.e. that ranges between +1 > 0) indicates a positive relationship.

Figure 6.1: *Scatterplots depicting three possible types of bivariate relationships*

6.1a: A positive relationship between participants' height and weight

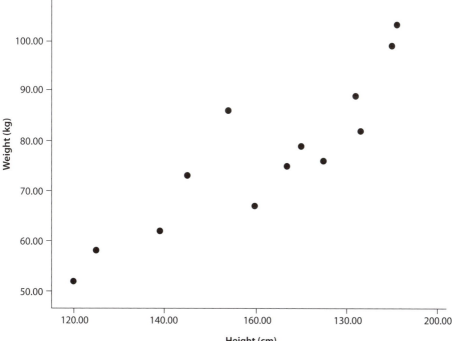

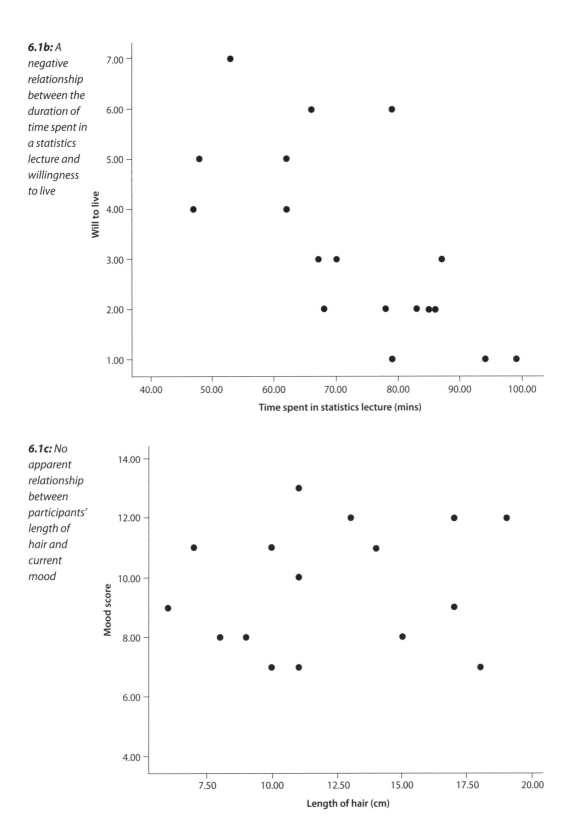

6.1b: *A negative relationship between the duration of time spent in a statistics lecture and willingness to live*

6.1c: *No apparent relationship between participants' length of hair and current mood*

In stark contrast to this, the data in Figure 6.1b shows an opposing trend of a **negative relationship**. Here we are plotting participants' 'will to live' against time spent in a statistics lecture. The overall pattern is for the dots to line up from the top left to the bottom right of the scatterplot – this means that as the length of time spent in a statistics lecture increases, scores on the 'will to live' metric actually decrease (does this ring true to you?) Perhaps unsurprisingly, any coefficient that has a negative value (i.e. that ranges between -1 and 0) indicates a negative relationship between the two variables.

Finally in Figure 6.1c, the scatterplot is depicting no clear relationship between the variables of hair length and current mood. Perhaps this comes as no surprise. Here we have two variables with no obvious connection between them – indeed, the dots appear to be randomly dispersed. The only linear trend we might be able to discern would be a thick horizontal one running left to right – but only if we scrunch up our eyes and squint at the plot! This apparently random pattern (and subsequent flat line) would indicate that there is no relationship between our two variables – as hair length gets longer, mood scores fluctuate in a haphazard manner. No doubt by now you will have guessed that a value of 0 indicates there is no relationship between the variables!

Task — Go back to the Task on page 82 and read over the list of paired variables. This time, try to identify the direction of the relationship between these variables.

Strength of relationship

As previously suggested, the correlation coefficient can also be used to determine the magnitude of this relationship, i.e. the strength of the association between these two variables. This strength is denoted by the relative size of the coefficient: ±0.1 indicates a weak relationship; ±0.3 indicates a moderate relationship; ±0.5 a strong relationship. (See Cohen (1988) for a discussion of these sizes.)

The display of coefficient sizes in Figure 6.2 should demonstrate that positive and negative coefficients are mirror images of each other. Identical coefficients share the same strength of association between variables, but the ± prefix merely indicates the direction of this association. It is also possible to observe in these figures that the data points (black dots) start to drift away from the line of best fit as the correlation coefficient (the magnitude of the association between the two variables) gets smaller.

Correlation ≠ causation

The invalid assumption that correlation implies cause is probably among the two or three most serious and common errors of human reasoning.

Stephen Jay Gould (1996, p272)

Figure 6.2: *Visual depiction of correlation magnitudes*

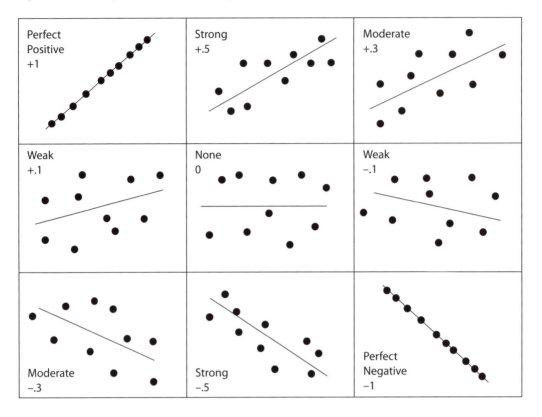

It is absolutely vital to remember that a correlation can only tell us about the degree of association between two variables – in no way, shape or form does it give any indication as to the cause of this relationship. This is something we always drill into students when teaching correlation. While undoubtedly there is a positive relationship between the size of a goldfish bowl and the number of goldfish contained within it, we cannot infer that it is the size of the bowl itself that has 'caused' the number of goldfish present. It would seem equally absurd to consider the opposite inter-pretation – that the number of goldfish has caused the size of the fish bowl. We can't say one caused the other. However, in effect, this is what we would be stating if we were to make a causal inference from a correlation. Remember, we are only measuring the degree of association between the number of goldfish and the size of the bowl; any cause-and-effect interpretations would be erroneous.

Other uses: reliability and validity

The correlational design has a number of uses in a research format. However, it has also proved to be extremely useful in two other areas that were introduced in Chapter 1 – reliability and validity.

These two constructs are a fundamental basis of research. Without reliability, we have no way to determine how 'accurate' our measures and techniques are in capturing the focus of our research. Without validity, we cannot be confident that the very thing we are proposing to measure is actually being measured. We might inadvertently be measuring some other related or possibly distinct construct.

Using a correlational design can assist with generating indices of reliability and validity in research. Classic examples of this in research include the use of questionnaires. Imagine you have just devised a brand-new questionnaire that measures depression. How do you know if it is reliable or valid? Some of the items (questions) might be quite poor at discriminating people who are depressed from those who are not; some items might not relate to depression at all. There are certain exercises we can undertake in order to assess its reliability and validity by virtue of a correlational design (see Table 6.1 for a summary of these).

Table 6.1: *Methods for obtaining correlation-based indices of reliability and validity*

Measure of reliability	What it is looking for	How to do it
Test-retest	Consistency of responses	Administer the task, and then at some later point (days/weeks/months) give the same task again and correlate both scores.
Inter-rater	Whether task is used in same manner by all researchers	Two researchers administer the task simultaneously to participants – correlate the scores on both tests.
Alternate/parallel	To avoid carry-over effects from repeated testing – alternate version of same task should produce consistent responses	Administer both versions of the test to participants and then correlate the two sets of scores.
Inter-item	Whether items on questionnaire are consistent	Correlate all the items on a questionnaire with each other and average these.
Split-half	As above	Split the questionnaire in two (for example, first half versus second half; odds versus evens) and correlate both halves.
Cronbach's alpha	Whether all items on questionnaire measure the same construct	Essentially a combination of inter-item and split-half reliability. SPSS can do this analysis.

Table 6.1: Continued

Measure of validity	What it is looking for	How to do it
Concurrent	Whether this task generates consistent responses compared to another task measuring the same construct (for example, Hamilton Depression Rating Scale and Beck Depression Inventory)	Administer one task and an existing task to participants – correlate the total scores on both of these tasks.
Predictive	Whether scores on this task can be used to predict performance on another task (for example, 11-plus exam and GCSE performance)	Similar to **concurrent validity** – see section on **regression** below (pages 88–90).

Task —— Consider the various methods that can provide measures of reliability and validity outlined in Table 6.1. As they are all based on the correlation coefficient, if your tasks were highly reliable and valid, why would you expect to see a positive correlation?

What happens if you have a third variable?

Conducting an investigation and only collecting data on two variables would be considered extremely myopic! It is unlikely that you can capture the complexity of interplay and the dynamics of a relationship between two variables without recourse to recording other measures as well. They may well have an impact on the relationship between your two variables (good or bad), but you would simply be unaware of this – at least until someone points it out to you. An example often trotted out in correlation lectures is the apparent (and noted) relationship between the declining local stork population and lowering birth rates. It is true! Many studies have shown such a relationship (read the very short paper by Matthews (2000), in which he succinctly demonstrates this), which seems to provide supportive evidence to the old wives' tale. Yet if we only measure two variables we appear to have stumbled across a genuine relationship between storks and birth rates, and do not consider the influence of a third (or more) variable(s).

Two examples of these third variables influencing a relationship are **moderator** and **mediator variables**. Simply put, a moderator variable exerts influence over the magnitude of a relationship between two other variables, while a mediator variable explains why the relationship between the two other variables exists. An excellent illustration of this concept can be seen on a website available for free viewing hosted by the University of Wisconsin-Madison (see Further reading, page 96). The authors ask you to consider the fictional results of a study investigating the relationship between socioeconomic status and the frequency of breast self-examinations in women. They conjecture that age might be a moderator variable as the relationship between social class and the frequency of self-examination could be stronger for older women and conversely weaker for younger women. They also posit that the level of education attained might act as a mediator variable: it may explain why there is a relationship between social class and the frequency of examination – when the effect of education level is partialled out (removed), the relationship between class and self-examinations disappears.

Using correlations to predict scores

An extension of this correlation technique is regression. A research study utilising regression uses the same basic design as a correlation study – it is also used to assess the degree of association between variables. However, it has additional benefits. You are no longer limited to studying just two variables, and now you can predict scores on one variable when given the values of another (or others).

Look at Figure 6.3. This scatterplot is a representation of the positive relationship between the annual take-home salary and the level of happiness of a sample of participants. Again, we have superimposed a line of best fit on to this plot – remember this is the best indicator of the linear trend of scores on both measures and the slope of this line represents the correlation coefficient itself. In regression, it is possible to predict how happy someone is likely to be given their annual salary (or vice versa). The statistical calculations involved in this procedure are beyond the scope of this chapter (see Further reading, pages 95–6), but are surprisingly straightforward to interpret.

We can use the scatterplot to visually represent the regression analysis. Let's imagine we have a participant who earns £40k per annum – from a quick back-of-a-beer-mat calculation we could draw a line straight up from the £40k on the salary axis until it reaches the line of best fit, and then continue horizontally until it reaches the happiness axis where we obtain a predicted happiness figure of about 15. The actual statistical procedure will, of course, provide a more accurate calculation – don't start using rulers in your lab sessions.

We may decide, however, that happiness is too complex an emotion to try to accurately predict scores on this from just annual salary – we could be accused of over-simplification. We may therefore wish to include multiple variables (such as quality of home life, size of family, stress measures, general health scores and so forth) and enter these into our analysis. The same process would apply, but it would be nigh on impossible to demonstrate this graphically as we would need a six-dimensional scatterplot at least!

Figure 6.3: Scatterplot used to predict level of happiness from annual salary (£k)

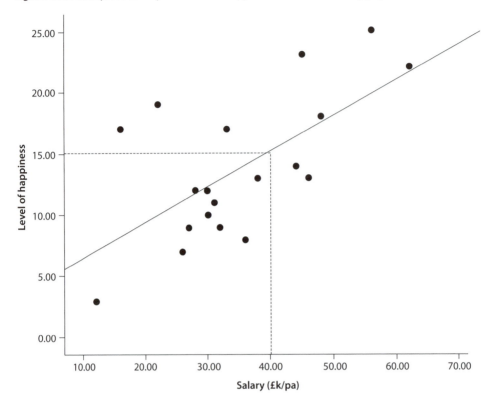

Non-linear relationships

So far, we have only described the method for investigating the linear relationship between variables. However, sometimes relationships between variables are just not that straightforward. An example commonly used to illustrate this is the link between anxiety and performance (say in an exam). As can be seen in Figure 6.4 below, the overall relationship between anxiety and exam performance is curvilinear. A simple interpretation of increasing anxiety being associated with increased exam performance would only explain the first half of the graph – increasingly higher levels of anxiety then become associated with lower exam scores. Such data is not untypical and can be analysed with more advanced correlation statistical techniques.

Figure 6.4: *Scatterplot of a curvilinear relationship between anxiety and exam scores*

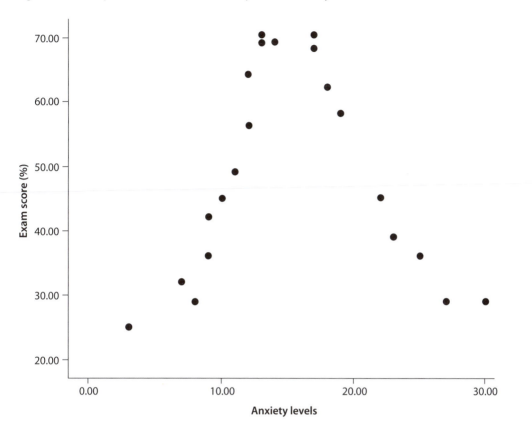

Critical thinking activity

Degree of association

Critical thinking focus: critical and creative thinking

Key question: *What is the point of using correlational designs in research?*

We conduct research in an attempt to learn more about a given topic. We may have constructed theories and models of how processes work, and what variables and factors influence our behaviours and responses on the basis of data collected from research. In order to keenly understand the specific weightings and relative impact these variables may have, we conduct experiments to study the effect of deliberate manipulations of these variables on our measures. This is the basic premise of experimental research. However, you have now been introduced to the correlational research design, which is not capable of lending weight to any elucidation of causal inferences among our variables. What then, is the point of this type of design in psychological research? Can it really further our knowledge of a given topic?

Consider the following questions to aid your critical appraisal.

1. Is all research predicated on demonstrating cause and effect?

2. Is demonstrating an association between variables actually helpful?

3. Might variables associate even though they share no basis for doing so?

Critical thinking review

This activity helps develop your skills of creative and critical thinking in relation to the use of correlational design. While this design is unable to provide any assessment of causal inferences, it permits alternative questions about variables to be asked. Rather than investigating differences in scores between experimental conditions, it focuses on the degree of association between variables – or conversely, the degree of independence between variables. This exercise should have helped you to critically evaluate the unique contribution that correlational design can bring to research; it provides a unique method of gathering information about the relationship between variables involved in any given field of study. Any additional information that is learned is always constructive.

Skill builder activity

Concurrent validity

Transferable skill focus: problem-solving

Key question: *Aaargh – why do I have a negative correlation?*

In Table 6.1 on pages 87–8 and in the Task immediately after, you were shown how the correlational design can be used to provide various measures of reliability and validity. If a task (such as a questionnaire) was highly consistent within itself, and was deemed to be very reliable and valid, then you would expect to see a correlation coefficient that was positive and very high (close to +1). Occasionally, however, when assessing the measures of validity previously described, you may occasionally find you have a high negative correlation instead.

To illustrate, suppose we have just designed a new questionnaire on anxiety and we wish to determine if it is consistent with a well-established and validated anxiety questionnaire. We give both questionnaires to our participants (see Tables 6.2a and 6.2b below), add up the total scores and conduct a correlation to assess the concurrent validity.

Table 6.2a: *Items from our new questionnaire on anxiety*

Q1. I am easily embarrassed in social situations.				
Q2. I tend to avoid busy crowds.				
Q3. I work best on my own.				
Q4. . . .				
Strongly disagree	**Disagree**	**Neither agree nor disagree**	**Agree**	**Strongly agree**
1	2	3	4	5

Table 6.2b: *Items from the existing anxiety questionnaire*

Q1. I find social events uncomfortable.				
Q2. I prefer my own company to that of others.				
Q3. I prefer to work alone.				
Q4. . . .				
Strongly agree	**Agree**	**Neither agree nor disagree**	**Disagree**	**Strongly disagree**
1	2	3	4	5

It is highly probable that we would find a negative correlation between these two questionnaires. This does not signify that there is no relationship between our two questionnaires – just the opposite. What then, do you think might explain this apparent paradox?

Hint: Consider the direction of the scoring scale on both questionnaires.

Skill builder review

Negative associations between variables can often be misinterpreted, and may initially be confusing for students in the context of measures of validity in research. This does not need to be the case – remember that a negative correlation merely indicates the direction of the relationship between scores on both variables: as one increases the other decreases. In the example of the two anxiety questionnaires, it should be immediately apparent that the scoring scales are in opposing directions. People who are socially anxious are likely to score higher on our questionnaire, but they will score lower on the existing questionnaire. Therefore, if both questionnaires are good measures of anxiety, you would expect them to correlate negatively in order to reflect this.

This quick activity has been designed to assist in the development of your problem-solving skills. As has been pointed out in Chapter 4 (and also see Chapter 11), we often encounter problems in research. While good planning can avoid most of these, occasionally problems or difficulties may present themselves, and it is of crucial importance that you are flexible and analytical enough to pinpoint these and adapt as necessary. This activity encouraged you to think through the issues and possible problems associated with the concurrent validity of a newly designed questionnaire – a task you should be familiar with in psychological research.

Assignments

1. We have specifically pointed out that this correlational design is used exclusively to assess the degree of association between two (or more) variables. It is not looking at differences between scores, and therefore produces no information about the cause-and-effect relationship between these variables. However, it is true to say that without a significant correlation coefficient, then no relationship exists between the variables. What are the implications of this statement?

2. Any conclusions that you may draw from a study involving the association between two variables might be at risk due to the influence of other variables. Therefore, researchers will often measure other variables and partial their effects out, i.e. attempt to remove their influence on the other variables. If you conducted such a study, how would you decide which other variables to collect – what would you need to consider in order to select such variables?

3. An extremely useful extension of researching the degree of association between variables is the ability to predict future scores. This may be a new concept to you in research methodology, but what do you think are the possible benefits of this approach? Can you foresee any limitations?

Summary: what you have learned

In this chapter, you were introduced to another type of design often used in research – the correlation. However, unlike the experimental designs presented in the preceding chapters, studies that use correlation are not investigating the causal relationship between variables – no variables are being actively manipulated. Instead, this research design helps us to investigate the degree of association between two (or more) variables. People often confuse correlational designs with repeated-measures (within-participant) designs. This is because in both designs participants are tested on the tasks on numerous occasions; however, correlated designs do not require the same tasks to be completed – it is possible to study the association between different tasks or variables!

We discussed how the associations between two variables can be visually represented by using a scatterplot. This helps to demonstrate any linear trends in the data. This association can be measured with a correlation coefficient – a figure that lies somewhere between ±1 and 0. This serves two purposes: it shows the direction of the relationship (positive, negative or none) and also the strength of this relationship (weak, medium or strong).

You should be able to appreciate the intricacies of the correlational design, and how it can be extended to provide valuable measures of reliability and validity. Furthermore, you were presented with the scenario of how moderating and mediating variables may influence the association between your two variables of interest. We also discussed the ability to use this linear trend to permit the prediction of scores.

By reading this chapter and completing all the tasks, assignments and exercises, you have further developed your knowledge of research designs and how to implement these. In addition, your creative-thinking and problem-solving abilities were tested by setting issues often faced by researchers. These are key ingredients for your skills as a psychologist, whether you wish to pursue a career in research or not.

Further reading

Baron, RM and Kenny, DA (1986) The Moderator-Mediator Variable Distinction in Social Psychological Research: Conceptual, Strategic, and Statistical Considerations. *Journal of Personality and Social Psychology*, 51(6), 1173–1182.

One of the original and most widely cited papers on moderating and mediating variables in psychological research. If you like a challenge this is highly recommended.

Cohen, J (1988) *Statistical Power Analysis for the Behavioral Sciences*. 2nd edition. Hillsdale, NJ: Lawrence Erlbaum Associates.

All you ever needed to know about statistical power!

Dancey, C and Reidy, J (2011) *Statistics Without Maths for Psychology*. 5th edition. Harlow: Prentice Hall.

Interested readers (or if you have to study statistics!) should consult this book to help with any statistical issues to which we have referred. Statistics can feel like an impenetrable subject at the best of times, but this book manages to strip away the scary equations and formula in order to get to grips with how to conduct and interpret statistics. Highly recommended.

Matthews, R (2000) Storks deliver babies (p=0.008). *Teaching Statistics*, 22(2), 36–38.

A devilishly simple illustration of how misusing correlations can lead to profoundly incorrect conclusions.

University of Wisconsin-Madison (last updated 1999) *Mediator Versus Moderator Variables.* Available online at http://psych.wisc.edu/henriques/mediator.html

An excellent précis of mediator and moderator variables.

Chapter 7

Introducing qualitative design

Learning outcomes

The purpose of this chapter is to introduce you to the basics of designing qualitative research. This chapter will help you to understand what qualitative methods are, as well as the strengths and weaknesses of qualitative design. Qualitative data collection and analysis are important skills in your studies and this chapter will form part of the foundation of your understanding. In Chapter 10, you will be introduced to the idea of **mixed methods** designs, which use both qualitative and quantitative methods. This chapter should help you to understand what qualitative methods offer as a way of understanding complex phenomena. We recommend that you use this chapter as groundwork for planning, conducting and discussing qualitative research during your undergraduate degree.

By the end of this chapter, you should:

- *comprehend the basis of qualitative design;*
- *understand the types of qualitative data collected;*
- *be able to recognise what qualitative research can and cannot do;*
- *be able to identify the strengths and weaknesses of qualitative design.*

Introduction

Every year, when I teach qualitative methods, a few students will say that they are looking forward to the qualitative methods module. When I ask them why, they say that they hate statistics because they are difficult. However, by the end of the qualitative methods module they usually say that qualitative methods are much harder than they thought they would be. But there are also students who tell me how much they love the qualitative approach. These students say that they find qualitative methods fulfilling and enlightening. Qualitative methods are not the easy option and they are not a shortcut. Those of us who use qualitative methods don't mind the work involved. We use them because we are passionate about them and also about the insights they can provide.

What are qualitative methods and what are they used for? There is no single thing that defines qualitative methods, other than they are not quantitative. That may seem obvious, but the term qualitative methods includes so much that it would be impossible to cover everything in these few short chapters. In these qualitative chapters (Chapters 7 to 9), you will get some guidance on what qualitative methods are, the kind of data collected and some of the ways that it is analysed.

The qualitative methods that you will be reading about in this book are the kind of thing that you are likely to experience during your undergraduate studies. So I won't bore you by going on at length about the philosophy and the epistemological origins of qualitative methods. If, at a later stage, you want to specialise in qualitative methods, then the philosophy is something that you will want to investigate and fully understand. What you do need to remember is that the various qualitative methods tend to come from a theoretical background. In other words, while the methods may look very similar, they have very different origins and focuses. For example, discourse analysis and grounded theory would present different perspectives on the same piece of data.

What are the strengths and weaknesses of qualitative methods?

Aside from the numbers, what is the difference between qualitative and quantitative methods? Well, to put it simply, quantitative methods can show us the 'what'; they can show us the phenomenon and how prevalent it is, and what it may be correlated to. That is great, but there are limits to this. Qualitative methods are not about showing how common something is; they are about looking at the quality of the phenomenon or experience. What they are looking at is the 'why'. Qualitative methods are concerned with a more in-depth understanding of data. We can use qualitative methods to go beyond the limits of questionnaires or experiments and ask more searching questions of our participants. Rather than giving participants four lines to write about their feelings or impressions of something, we can give them the space and time to tell us everything they want to. We can ask additional questions to get them to expand their responses when this is appropriate or when we hear an interesting comment that we would like to understand more fully. Probably the most important strength of qualitative methods is how good they are at looking at 'real-world' situations. So, rather than looking at something in a laboratory or giving people questionnaires to complete, we can use qualitative methods to look at things as they happen. To give you an example, you can think about how you would look at persuasion and how various persuasion strategies affect people. You could devise a laboratory experiment that gets participants to give responses to persuasion techniques. You could create a questionnaire that asks people about how persuasive they found various strategies. Alternatively, you could use qualitative interviews to ask people about the strategies themselves, how these made them feel and how these guided their responses. Which of these do you think would give you a better insight into how persuasion works?

However, the strengths of qualitative methods can also be their limitations. Qualitative methods are in-depth, so they produce large amounts of data and can be very time-consuming to carry out.

The analytic methods are also often time-consuming; no clicking the right options and getting the answer as there is with SPSS. Instead, there are likely to be weeks, or even months, of hard work. The findings of qualitative methods cannot be extrapolated across a population. They give a snapshot of a particular participant or phenomenon, but they cannot show whether that snapshot can be seen beyond the boundaries of that study. Qualitative methods cannot give *the* answer, they give *an* answer. The analysis is interpretative in nature so if five qualitative analysts examined the same piece of data they would probably produce five different analyses. All of these analyses would also be correct, provided they could cite evidence to support their findings.

You need to remember what you read earlier on – research methods are a toolkit. You need to select the right tool for the right job, and you shouldn't criticise the tool because it cannot do the job you want it to. Qualitative methods will not help you much if you are interested in attentional interference. However, on the other hand, an experiment cannot tell you much about someone's experience of bereavement. If you pick the wrong method to examine something, then you are trying to knock a nail in with a screwdriver – you can just about do it, but not only is it inefficient, it's also far more difficult than if you had chosen the hammer.

Task —— Which methods do you think would be most suitable to investigate the following topics? Consider how you could gain the deepest and most appropriate understanding of these topics.

– People's fear of crime.

– Study habits in students.

– 'Celebrity' magazines and body image.

Are quantitative methods better than qualitative?

One of the comments I hear from students is that qualitative methods aren't 'proper psychology'; that they are 'woolly' or 'fuzzy', or that they lack reliability. If you are a great fan of quantitative methods you have probably thought of some of these criticisms yourself. Much of your introductory studies in psychology are likely to have been based on studies using traditional experimental methods. Consequently, if that is what you have been taught psychology is all about, the qualitative methods may well look problematic. So let's deal with these criticisms one by one.

Qualitative methods aren't 'proper psychology' – Well, aside from asking what you mean by 'proper psychology', this comment tends to be informed by a rather old-fashioned idea of psychology. This idea is that only things you can quantify are worth examining. However, think about psychology in practice, such as that employed by a clinical psychologist. When they are evaluating a patient, they don't use a five point Likert scale and they do not use a fixed response questionnaire. They use a series of semi-structured questions and have the potential to ask more questions if something arises that they think needs further examination. The clinical process is a qualitative one, informed and supported by quantitatively examined diagnostic materials rather than experimental techniques.

Some of the methods we use in the qualitative field also look very unlike those you've probably come across before. Qualitative observation looks about as far removed from quantitative methods as you can get. We will be looking at this in more detail in Chapter 8, but qualitative observation is a way of looking at how people interact in a specific situation or context and recording very detailed information about the participant's behaviour. It is tempting to use a tick sheet when utilising this method and just count how many times the participant does a particular action. However, this isn't a qualitative observation and it lacks the depth that the data can actually provide when considered fully. So what might you use this for? It is particularly useful for gathering data from participants who cannot answer questions, such as pre-verbal children, or for examining group behaviours.

Qualitative methods are 'fuzzy' – To say that qualitative methods are not an exact and absolute science is a valid statement. Qualitative methods are not strictly regimented and controlled in the same way as a laboratory experiment or similar techniques. However, you could ask why every method should be so rigorously controlled. The nature of strictly structured experiments or surveys is that they only allow a limited range of responses. In contrast, qualitative methods allow participants a greater degree of freedom in their responses. They also allow them to give you data that is potentially more representative than a quantitative method can. It must be acknowledged that both quantitative and qualitative methods can be fuzzy if poorly designed or conducted. However, one of the things that we do in qualitative methods is to ensure that we are as systematic in our approach as possible. It is also important to remember that qualitative researchers maintain an awareness of how their own beliefs and values influence their choice of research design and interpretation of data. This principle is called reflexivity and is present in most qualitative designs. It is also in direct comparison to quantitative designs, which state that the researcher should aim to be objective. In Chapters 8 and 9 you will be introduced to how qualitative data are gathered and analysed. This will show you how to take a systematic qualitative approach and will also help you to learn ways in which you can ensure that your qualitative studies are not fuzzy.

Qualitative methods lack reliability – This is a criticism that is often levelled at qualitative methods and, to some extent, it is true. After all, with quantitative methods you would aim to have a large representative sample, so that you could show that the results were significant and reliable, and could be extrapolated across a population. In theory, if you were to get another representative sample you would get the same result, or one which is very close to it. But qualitative methods do not claim to show significance, nor do they set out to show that something can be extrapolated across a population. It is even argued in qualitative methods that the notion of reliability is problematic. To assume that anyone can replicate a study and get the same results requires the design to be based around a very fixed framework. Instead, I could counter this argument by saying that although qualitative methods may lack reliability, they have far greater validity than quantitative methods when looking at the same thing. To give you an example, if you were asked to design a study to look at students' experience of Freshers' Week, which techniques would you use? You would need to identify things, such as whether the participants enjoyed the process, whether they found it a positive experience, and if it helped them to make new friends. You could use a questionnaire with questions such as 'How much did you enjoy Freshers' Week?' and ask participants to select points on Likert scales that reflect their opinions. Presumably, if you asked a large enough sample of students, you would hopefully get some significant results. However, a design like this does not really tell you very much and does not provide sufficient depth of knowledge. It may be more appropriate to ask participants about their experiences, what they liked and didn't like, and what would have improved the experience. After all, they may have liked some parts of Freshers' Week and hated others. So asking a simple 'How much did you like it?' question doesn't really explore the full scope of the participants' experiences. It could be argued that the qualitative approach actually examines the experiences in a more valid manner than the quantitative.

The qualitative methods you need to know

There is a huge variety of qualitative methods. Some of these are very simple while others are much more complex and challenging. It would take a much longer book than this to take you through all of them, but further reading is suggested at the end of this chapter (see page 109). In this book, you will be looking at some of the most used qualitative methods. Also, and more importantly, you will be looking at the methods that are accessible to undergraduate students. Qualitative methods encompass both data collection and data analysis, and it is important to remember that qualitative analysis only works efficiently on qualitative data.

The qualitative methods we will be covering in this book are:

- data collection methods

  - observation data;

  - interview data;

  - focus group data;

  - naturally occurring data;

- data analysis methods

  - grounded theory

  - thematic analysis

  - discourse analysis.

These different approaches will help you in both your research methods and also as you read studies that use these methods. By understanding how the studies are carried out, you will be able to take a more critical stance in evaluating them.

Designing a qualitative study

The process of designing a qualitative study starts with a research question, which, depending on what that question is, leads us to methods of data collection and analysis. The data collection method is also determined by the methods of analysis. This probably all sounds rather complicated, but it will become clear. In many ways, it is not so different from the quantitative approach; you know what you are interested in and that will dictate how you are going to gather the data and what you are going to do with it. However, it is important to remember that the three methods of qualitative data analysis that you are going to read about in this book may look very similar to you, but they all come from different theoretical perspectives. As such, the type of data you collect and your research question will both play a significant role in determining which analysis you should use.

Why are there no hypotheses?

You will be used to generating a hypothesis and null hypothesis from your quantitative studies, but students are often confused by qualitative design because there are no explicitly stated hypotheses. A hypothesis is, as you may know, the proposition that is tested in quantitative research. Whether this hypothesis is supported or not depends entirely on the level of statistical significance observed during quantitative analyses. Instead, we devise research questions. The research question is the thing that we are interested in – for example, students' experiences of Freshers' Week. We are not looking to prove what students enjoy most about Freshers' Week. Instead, we are aiming to get an impression of those participants' experiences and to systematically interrogate the data to reach our findings.

So what is the key difference between a hypothesis and a research question? To put it simply, with a hypothesis we are making some kind of a prediction about our results. But with a research question we are not trying to predict what we are going to get; we are just saying what we are interested in.

How do you develop a research question?

This is the first stage in a qualitative study and although you may well have a general idea about what you are interested in, you may not understand how to translate that into a workable research question. One of the main flaws in research questions is that they are too large to be manageable. The big questions are a good place to start, but then you need to refine them from there. So you start big and then narrow your topic down to something that is possible within the timeframe and resources available to you. You also need to think about how it fits into psychology. To give you an example, you may be interested in the social construction of gender. That is a huge question to tackle and entire books have been written about it. This really isn't a manageable research question in its current state. To make it more manageable, you need to think about reducing it to something more specific. Rather than trying to research the social construction of gender as a whole, you might like to think about the social construction of gender in relation to something like young people's expectations of career paths. That would give you the scope to talk to students about what they think men's and women's career paths may be and the impact of taking time to raise children or care for relatives. This would give some insight into the social construction of gender roles and would relate to gender psychology in your study. By moving from a really big area to something much more specific, you can produce research with greater depth and clarity. As I was always told when I was a student, it is better to write a lot about a little, than a little about a lot.

Sampling

When you design a qualitative research project, you need to think about sampling in a slightly different manner than when you design a quantitative design. You have already learnt about sampling to gain a representative sample, and one that is sufficiently large that your findings will be considered rigorous enough. In contrast to the possible hundreds of participants for quantitative designs, in qualitative designs you are likely to have much smaller samples. The question of how many participants you will need depends very much on what you are doing, but you will read more about this in Chapter 8 on qualitative data collection. The most important aspect of sampling for qualitative methods is that they are purposive – that is to say, you seek out participants who are suitable for the research you are doing. So you would find people who had experience of the thing you are interested in or opinions regarding it. One of the sampling techniques that is really useful in qualitative methods is the snowball technique. Snowball sampling works on the basis that people often know others who have similar experiences to themselves, and they will probably know more people like themselves than you do. If you wanted to interview a very specific group of people, stay-at-home dads, for example, you might find one man to interview but he is quite likely to know other men who are also stay-at-home dads. So by finding one person, you can often find more. The snowball technique is also very useful in quantitative methods and can provide you with a sufficient sample in a very quick time.

Task — If you wanted to find six participants to take part in interviews about experiences of coming out as gay in communities that are very opposed to homosexuality, what do you think would be the best way of finding them?

Qualitative methods and ethics

There are certain aspects of qualitative methods that mean you need to take a closer account of ethics than you may have to in quantitative designs. Obviously, with a questionnaire design, the participant is often anonymous. Indeed, you may not even ever meet the participant, making it unlikely that you could ever identify them. However, in qualitative research we need to think more carefully about ethics because we are asking participants for permission to look at them in some depth. This is also potentially problematic because we often use a much smaller number of participants than in quantitative studies. If you are doing an experimental study with 100 participants and one withdraws, that would not cause too great an effect. But if you are doing an interview study with six participants and one withdraws, this can have a very serious effect. This can be even worse with focus group designs. For example, if you have run a focus group and one participant decides to withdraw, you have to remove the entire data for that focus group. In order to ensure that participant withdrawal is kept to a minimum, you need to take care in the design and preparation of the data collection. We will look at this in more detail in Chapter 8.

Qualitative methods often use recording equipment, including both audio and video recording, during data gathering. The ethical implications of these data collection tools are something to keep in mind. This data is not like questionnaire or experimental data and is not easily anonymised in the same way. You must ensure that it is held securely and that it is not seen or heard by anyone who is not directly involved in the analysis. Usually, it will only be the researcher and their supervisor who will have access to the data in its raw form. It is important that the data is carefully protected at all times. As you will have seen in Chapter 2, qualitative studies often ask participants for intimate and personal information about their feelings and experiences. Therefore, you have a responsibility as the researcher to treat this data with great respect, and to keep it confidential and secure. After all, you wouldn't like someone to tell everyone what you had said in a private situation, would you?

In observation studies, we also need to think about ethics very carefully. Remember that people have a reasonable expectation of privacy in some public settings. So if you are conducting observation in a public place, you should take care not to breach that expectation of privacy. You will have read about Humphrey's tearoom trade study and the potentially serious consequences for the participants who had no opportunity to refuse consent or to withdraw. Remember that studies that use public observation should not cause harm or embarrassment to the participants. You may want to use observation with participants who can give consent, and who you gather together for the observation study. Observation is also great for studies involving children, as experiments with children can be very tricky, given children's ability (or lack thereof) to follow instructions. With observation studies, as you will see in Chapter 8, the use of video recording is very helpful. However, obviously, parents may feel uncomfortable about having their children videoed by someone, so it is vital to ensure that you treat such data with the upmost respect. As with all data, you need to think about the feelings and wishes of participants, and to try to maintain the highest ethical practice at all times.

Task — In qualitative methods we invite people to talk about their experiences and beliefs. Can you think of any situations when asking people about these things might be unethical?

Final considerations

Qualitative methods, when used well, can provide fascinating findings and deep insights into people's experiences and behaviour. But qualitative methods can be badly misused or misapplied. The skill with all research methods is to choose the correct methods of data collection and analysis for the phenomenon in which you are interested. Very often, the downfall of qualitative research is that the methods have been poorly chosen and applied. In Chapters 8 and 9, you will be learning more about the methods of data collection and analysis, and how we go about selecting the right tools for the job.

Critical thinking activity

The value of qualitative data

Critical thinking focus: analysing and evaluating

Key question: *How do qualitative methods measure up against quantitative methods?*

You have read that qualitative methods do not try to extrapolate from their findings to a general population. Think about the implications of this. Does this mean that the data and findings are inevitably weaker than those in quantitative methods?

Consider the following questions to aid your critical appraisal.

- What are the implications of only using quantitative methods?

- Are your own experiences less useful if they do not fit neatly into a quantitative measure?

- Do the phenomena that qualitative methods examine lend themselves to quantitative measures?

- How do we decide what constitutes a strong finding?

- If we treat quantitative methods as the 'gold standard' of research, can anything that doesn't fall into that category ever be regarded as sufficient?

Critical thinking review

The aim of this activity is to encourage you to think about qualitative methods as valid research methods in psychology. What is important to remember is that psychology is a huge discipline, and while many aspects are suited to quantitative measures, it is not sufficient for all psychological research. Within qualitative methods it is argued that the reliance on quantification and the traditional objective 'scientific' models of research relate to the desire for psychology to be regarded as a 'hard' science, like chemistry or physics. Qualitative methodologists would argue that human beings interpreting other human beings can never be entirely 'scientific', and should therefore aim to be systematic, while acknowledging the potentially subjective nature of ourselves in research (see Chapter 10).

Skill builder activity

Evaluating methodology selection

Transferable skill focus: independent learning

Key question: *Has the right method been chosen?*

In the Task on page 99, you were asked whether qualitative or quantitative methods would be more appropriate for examining several phenomena that can be studied in psychology. Go back to this task and think about this in more depth. For the three different phenomena, think about what the most suitable design would be and also identify why this would be the case. It might be useful to list and compare the strengths and weaknesses of both qualitative and quantitative methods in relation to each research topic. In this task, you are not expected to just assume quantitative methods should be used. You must critically discuss both qualitative and quantitative approaches before identifying which design you would use and why you would choose to study the phenomena in this way.

Skill builder review

This task is designed to encourage you to evaluate and argue for the most suitable methods for examining aspects of human behaviour:

- people's fear of crime

- study habits in students

- 'celebrity' magazines and body image.

Which method would be the most suitable, in your opinion, for each of these? Let's have a look at the first topic to give you an idea of how you could argue your position.

People's fear of crime is an issue that concerns not only psychologists, but also criminologists, politicians and the criminal justice system. It is often argued that fear of crime is far out of proportion to most people's risk of being a victim of crime. So how would you go about looking at fear of crime? From a quantitative perspective, you could do a large-scale questionnaire study, asking participants if they are afraid that they may be victims of crime. You could include all sorts of factors that we know are important in these studies: the participants' age, gender, where they live and their occupation. From this, we could find rates of fear of crime and compare them with actual crime statistics.

A qualitative study could carry out in-depth interviews about the fear of crime. It could ask about the kinds of crime that participants are frightened of, but also ask why they are afraid of those crimes. For example, do they know people who have been victims of crime? Does their fear of crime limit what they do or impact how they feel about things like public transport or going out late at night? It may also be insightful to ask how they know about certain crimes as their opinion may reflect media portrayal rather than personal experience. This could present significantly deeper and more insightful knowledge than quantitative approaches could provide.

The other two topics would also present possibilities from either perspective. For the study habits of students, you could look at how much time each participant spends studying, where they study and the methods they use. You could then compare this data with their results to gain a correlational finding. Alternatively, you could talk to them about how they study, and how effective they think of themselves as students. You could even do an observational study and look at how students study in the learning centre.

For the question of body image and 'celebrity magazines', you could survey people who read these magazines and measure them on a body image scale to find how they come out on these tests. You could find participants who have never read these magazines, test their body image, get them to read them for a couple of weeks, and then test their body image again. Alternatively, you could talk to participants about how these magazines make them feel. Often, when you talk to people about these magazines, they say that they know that pictures are photoshopped and they aren't real, but that doesn't seem to change how they feel about themselves.

For all of these topics, both qualitative and quantitative methods would give us a great deal of information, and there are strengths and weaknesses in both methods. This task should have helped you to think about the different methods and to see that making that decision is not a cut-and-dried process.

Summary: what you have learned

This chapter has introduced some of the key aspects of qualitative research methods. You should now be aware of the strengths and weaknesses of qualitative methods and the types of research for which qualitative methods are most suitable.

You have read about some of the main criticisms of qualitative methods. These include that they are not 'real' psychology, that they are unscientific and that they lack reliability. You should understand both sides to these arguments and the defences that qualitative methodologists offer to these criticisms. You should also understand that this debate is ongoing and unlikely to be resolved in the immediate future due to the complex and multifaceted nature of research.

By reading this chapter and completing the tasks within it, you should be on your way to understanding why we use qualitative methods and what they can contribute to our understanding of human behaviour and experience.

Assignments

1. You have been instructed to design a qualitative study for your psychology department to find out how the induction week for new students went. The department specifically wants to know

which activities the students enjoyed, which they did not enjoy, and what improvements could be made for next year. It would also like to know which factors are important in determining whether students stay at university or leave in their first term. You will need to think about how you are going to go about recruiting the participants, which qualitative design you will use, and what you are going to talk to them about.

2. Critically compare qualitative and quantitative designs with reference to examples of how these approaches have been employed in contemporary psychology. You will need to evaluate their key features, the insights that they have provided and their strengths and limitations. It may be useful to apply your argument to one or more areas of study. These can include any topic, but a few suggestions include group behaviour, relationships, obedience and conformity. For example, how useful are qualitative and quantitative approaches when examining these phenomena?

3. Evaluate the claim that qualitative designs are inferior to quantitative designs because they are unscientific, relative and unstructured. You are not expected to automatically agree or disagree with this proposition, but rather evenly consider and debate each side of the argument. You are also expected to draw your own conclusions based on this debate and evidence provided by other literature.

Further reading

Howitt, D (2010) *Introduction to Qualitative Methods in Psychology*. Harlow: Prentice Hall.

A comprehensive and readable book covering qualitative methods, data collection and analysis.

Silverman, D (2006) *Interpreting Qualitative Data*. 3rd edition. London: Sage.

This text contains student-friendly sections concerning qualitative design.

Chapter 8

Qualitative data collection

Learning outcomes

The purpose of this chapter is to introduce you to some of the types of qualitative data and how to collect them.

By the end of this chapter you will be able to:

- *select the most suitable type of data and how to collect it;*
- *design the structure of the data collection;*
- *record your data;*
- *prepare your data for analysis.*

Introduction

So you've decided that your research requires a qualitative method and you know what you are interested in. Now what do you do? This chapter is going to take you through the main steps in planning and collecting your data and preparing it for analysis.

Observation

Planning and carrying out observation requires some preparation. What are you going to observe and where are you going to observe it? Whatever observation you carry out, you will be aiming to produce a set of **field notes**. The field notes you produce for observation studies should be as clear and comprehensive as they can be. When you are writing them, think about it as if you were giving an account to someone who wasn't there. Would they have a good idea of what had happened from your notes?

The two forms that you are going to read about here are naturalistic and laboratory observations. In naturalistic observation, you are observing people in a public place. Because people are aware that they are in a public place, you do not need to gain consent before you start. This does come with a couple of caveats: you should not record people's speech and you should be aware of situations when people would have a reasonable expectation of privacy, even in a public place – for example, in changing rooms, toilets and phone boxes. Think about which places you would feel were private in a public place. Laboratory observation is where your participants are aware that they are being observed – whether they have been brought into a laboratory environment, or you have gone into someone's environment and are potentially manipulating some aspect of it. In this form of observation, you must gain consent from your participants.

Let's take the naturalistic observation first: you are going to observe in a public place, where people would have a reasonable expectation of being watched. Before you start out, you should have a pretty good idea of what you are going to see; this will help as you make your notes. It is useful to take a while just to watch what is going on and the kind of behaviours you are seeing. Once you have done this, you can make a set of shorthand notes for these common behaviours. Then you can make a start.

Task —| Have a go at observation in a public place – somewhere like a coffee shop or a train station. Give yourself a few minutes to watch people and design some shorthand. Now write observation notes for a five-minute observation period. Do you think your notes are accurate?

When you read your notes back from the Task, they probably look a bit patchy, but this is not uncommon. One tactic that students sometimes employ is to use a ticksheet – how many times do people do something. While this does make it easier to record actions, it doesn't give a very clear or full description of the observation. So how can you make your field notes better? Practice is one thing; the more you carry out observations, the better you become. Another way that observation notes can be made better is to utilise **inter-coder reliability**. This is where two or more people carry out the observation, and then compare notes. Provided both observers have noted the same action, then it stays in the notes; if only one observer notes it, then it is rejected. By using inter-coder reliability, it allows you to record well-evidenced data (see Chapter 6).

As you've probably realised, this kind of observation is quite challenging and possibly is not suited to producing very detailed field notes. It can show quite general behaviours, and is useful for watching large crowds and behaviours around specific environments. A good alternative to naturalistic observation is laboratory observation. In this type of observation, you can control the environment and, importantly, you can record behaviour. By videoing the observation, you can relax about your field notes; you will be able to watch the behaviour over and over again. Obviously, as this is videoed, you must gain consent from the participants, and they should be made aware that they are going to be filmed.

What kind of situation lends itself to laboratory observation? To be honest, the only limit is your imagination. You could video children playing with a new toy or a group of strangers trying to solve a puzzle that requires them to cooperate.

Task —— Find a short video (YouTube is great for this, or you could use a news site such as the BBC). Watch it once, just to familiarise yourself with it and then make a set of field notes. Did you get to a point where there was nothing else to write, or did you find that every time you watched, there was something else to write?

Interviews

One of the most common forms of data collection by qualitative methods is the one-to-one interview. Interviews are quick to carry out, and can give a great depth of data. They allow your participant to be frank and open in an intimate and non-judgemental setting. Interview technique is a useful skill to learn, and although your first few interviews might be a bit clunky, you will soon improve. The best way to think about an interview is as a guided conversation, with the participant being the main speaker. It might seem obvious, but you don't want an interview where you are doing all the talking!

How do you go about preparing for a semi-structured interview? Unlike experiments, the preparations are fairly simple and you do not need terribly complicated equipment. Obviously, you need a participant, a recording device (most mp3 players and mobile phones have perfectly sensitive recording facilities), and an **interview schedule**. It is also important to have a suitable room in which to conduct the interview. It should be quiet and comfortable, and preferably somewhere that you are not likely to be disturbed.

You may have started with a very broad area of interest that you want to study, but it is important to determine what it is about that area that you would like to know more about. Interviews can give you a lot of information, but to provide rich data, you need to be thinking about how to narrow your field down to something suitable for an interview. If you try to cover too much in an interview, you won't get the depth of data that you want. You might be interested in people's experiences of education, but imagine that as an interview topic: do you ask them about starting school at five years old? Or what it was like to take exams for the first time? Or how they are coping with the differences between school and university? You need to focus down to something more specific. Reading the existing literature in this area will help; maybe there is something that sparks your interest that you would like to examine. Maybe you have found a gap in the literature and you would like to look at something that nobody seems to have discussed before. With this in mind, you can start creating an interview schedule.

What the success or failure of your interview really rests on is this interview schedule. The interview schedule is essentially a list of questions that you are going to ask. Don't think that the schedule is entirely fixed; in semi-structured interviews you can be flexible. You are able to rearrange the order of questions or ask other questions if your participant says something you would like to know more about. For a 20-minute interview you will probably need about seven questions. Most students, when they start interviewing, write too many questions and instead of letting the participant talk, they try to rush through their schedule. When you are drawing up your interview schedule, try not to write as if you are writing a questionnaire. If in doubt, read your questions critically. Could you answer your questions with one sentence? If so, then it is probably not phrased correctly. Here is an example: 'Did you enjoy school?' Your participant could just say 'yes' or 'no', which wouldn't be very informative. It would be better to phrase it as, 'What were your experiences of school like?' In this way, your participant has a wider scope to answer. You can also use prompt questions to encourage your participant. These are very useful to keep at hand during interviews; they are things like 'That's interesting, could you tell me some more about that?', or 'How did that make you feel?' These prompts encourage your participant to keep talking. Another question form that you should avoid is the double-barrelled question, asking two questions in one. Participants will often only answer one part of the question, which is frustrating, so ask two questions separately rather than asking a doubled question.

Task — Try writing a seven-question interview schedule about being a student. Think about the things that you would like your participant to talk about, and remember to read it critically to make sure you haven't asked any closed questions.

Once the interview schedule is written, it is useful to pilot it, just as you would a quantitative study. As you carry out the pilot, think about which questions work well and which don't. At any point, did your participant say that they didn't understand or didn't know how to answer? Take their comments on board and make changes to your schedule accordingly.

Now that you have an interview schedule that has been piloted, you can run your interviews. I don't need to tell you how to talk to people, but there are some guidelines that can help you to run interviews: be friendly and engaged; show your participant that you are listening; don't be aggressive or combative. Sometimes your participant may say something you strongly disagree with; bite your tongue and don't argue, just let them talk. What can be very difficult is that you want to join in and give your own experiences or thoughts. Remember, the interview isn't about you; it is about your participant.

Focus groups

You may have heard of focus groups in relation to market research, advertising or politics. The core idea of the focus group is that a group is gathered together and is asked to discuss a specific topic or area. Focus groups may seem rather intimidating at first; you've got to get a group together and then get them to talk to one another. What if it all goes wrong? Like interviews, the first focus group you run may well be slightly chaotic, but with preparation and a little practice, they do get much easier. Focus groups can also be really useful in the way that participants spark ideas off one another, giving you a range of data that you may not have gained in interviews.

In terms of preparation, focus groups are much like interviews. You will need participants, recording equipment and a focus group schedule. Given that you will have a number of people talking, possibly at the same time, recording equipment needs to be thought about more carefully. A digital recorder with an external microphone is better for sound pick-up, and using a video recorder is also helpful. When you need to transcribe, a video recording can help you to differentiate who is speaking if there is confusion on the voice recording. Your focus group schedule is going to be much like an interview schedule, posing questions and asking opinions.

Your role in the focus group is slightly different from that of the interviewer. You will act as the 'moderator' or 'facilitator' of the group. You ask the questions and try to keep the discussion flowing, but you will also need to keep the relationships within the group as cordial as possible. Sometimes, if you are running a group on a controversial topic, you may find that people become combative. Your role here is to try not to let things get out of hand. As in any group, a focus group may encounter group dynamics influenced by members of the group. One person may dominate the conversation, another may be very reticent; you will need to try to quieten and encourage them respectively. Just as in interviews, you may want to join in, but again, you need to listen and let the participants speak.

Naturally occurring data

Sometimes the most interesting data is naturally occurring. It would be difficult to carry out an interview or focus group that would tell you about how people interact in a seminar, but a recording of a seminar would be invaluable for that. Naturally occurring data uses recording equipment, and while all participants are aware of the recording, it doesn't ask participants to do anything beyond what they would normally be doing or saying in that environment. You might record family interactions at the breakfast table, a seminar or a job interview. Naturally occurring data gives scope for fascinating data. A great example is work using police interviews. Most of us have probably never been in a police interview, and we may only have heard one on the television. But imagine how fascinating it would be to be able to access those interviews. Kelly Benneworth had done just that and has analysed police interviews with child sex offenders (Benneworth, 2009). The data provided in these police interviews could not be gathered in any other way. The value of naturally occurring data like this is incalculable. And, like natural observation, the possibilities are endless. All you need is consent and well-placed recording equipment, and a world of data is available to you.

Preparing recorded data for analysis

Once you have your recorded data, be it interview, focus group or naturally occurring data, you will need to prepare it for analysis. Transcription is the process of creating an accurate written record of the data you have recorded. There are different levels of detail in transcription. The simplest form is a gloss transcription, which is where you tidy up the transcript, taking out pauses and overlapping speech, and type the language in standard English. Gloss transcriptions look rather like playscripts, and while they are tidy, they are not a terribly accurate representation of language interactions. The most useful form of transcription is one that was created for use in conversation analysis and discursive psychology; this is known as Jefferson transcription. This form of transcription was named after Gail Jefferson, who first laid out the transcription method and symbols to indicate the subtle aspects of speech: inflection, emphasis, laughter and other non-words. Jefferson transcription can be extremely complex, particularly for use in conversation analysis, but it is an adaptable system and you only need to make it as complex as it needs to be. For thematic analysis or grounded theory, you would use a very simple transcription, while for discursive psychology you would use a much more detailed transcription.

Here is a very brief glossary of transcription symbols.

[A left square bracket shows when overlapping speech starts.

] A right square bracket shows when overlapping speech stops.

= An equals sign shows where there is no gap between one person stopping speaking and the next person starting.

(0.0) Numbers in round brackets indicate the length of pauses in seconds and tenth of seconds.

(.) A full stop in round brackets indicate a pause of around a tenth of a second.

↑↓ Arrows up and down indicate rising and falling pitch or inflection.

? A question mark indicates something that sounds like a question.

_ Underlining shows emphasis of a word or a part of a word.

CAPITALS Capital letters show very strong or loud emphasis.

(( )) Double brackets indicates the transcriber's description. This might be laughing, a tone such as ((sarcastically)) or ((baby voice)). It can also be used to show that what has been said is inaudible.

Adapted from Jefferson (2004)

Transcription is a time-consuming process, but it serves to do more than produce a transcript. It also makes you intimately familiar with the data; by listening to it over and over again, you become very close to it. When you transcribe, don't try to get a fully detailed transcript down at the first go. Instead, first of all, just concentrate on getting the words down on the page. Once you have done that, then go back and start to include the symbols in your transcript. At this stage, you will probably spot mistakes in your initial transcript, and that you have been automatically tidying up the language used. You may find the process frustratingly slow at first, but you will soon start to speed up as you get used to transcribing.

Task — Find a clip of an interview or discussion on YouTube or the BBC news site. Have a go at transcribing it; first getting the words down, then adding the symbols and correcting your first attempt. How long did it take you? When you read your first transcription, how many mistakes did you make? Don't worry if you made a lot; everyone who does this work does. The important thing is to make sure you correct them.

Now you have got your data ready, collected and transcribed, you can start analysis. Remember to back up both your transcript and your raw data files; you've spent a lot of time on them, they are worth protecting.

Critical thinking activity

Evaluating the value of data

Critical thinking focus: analysing and evaluating

Key question: *Isn't naturally occurring data the most 'real'?*

In this chapter you have seen that data can be gathered either by generating a situation or question to examine a phenomenon, or by gathering data that occurs naturally. Is one form of data more valuable than the other?

Consider the following questions to aid your critical appraisal.

- You could argue that the data that you have generated are only responses to the stimuli that you have created. Is that really examining the phenomenon? Or is it simply gaining responses to your own interpretation of that phenomenon?

- Naturally occurring data shows you how people act and interact in a situation. We have all been in a situation when we were angry, frustrated or embarrassed, and we *wish* that we had had a witty riposte or a crushing put-down. But we didn't say that; we just wanted to. By recording the real interaction, we can see the way that people really act, not the way they wish they would.

Equally, you could argue that trying to gather data in a natural environment is limiting in that you can only examine what happens at that point in time, and that you cannot probe or stimulate more depth.

Think about when you meet someone and they ask, 'How are you?' You will usually say 'I'm fine, how are you?' Does that mean that you are fine, or that you may not be in a position or situation where you can give more depth?

By asking about feelings and experiences, can you not draw out the internal motivations and complexities of your participants?

Critical thinking review

The aim of this activity is to encourage you to think about data collection and what is most suitable. While the question of which data is more useful is ongoing, hopefully you have seen that both naturally occurring data and generated data are useful for different things. There isn't a one-size-fits-all approach to data collection and nor should there be.

Gathering data is flexible and should respond to the demands of the research question and approach. By sticking to a single method dogmatically, you may miss something valuable and informative. Moreover, data collection methods are increasing all the time – for example, there has been something of a boom in analysis of telephone interaction, made so much easier by modern telephone systems that allow clear recording. Who knows what the next innovation will be, but data collection methods should be open enough to adapt to meet those needs.

Skill builder activity

Designing studies in unfamiliar areas

Transferable skill focus: organisation skills

Key question: *How do you study something you don't know much about?*

You have decided to do a series of interviews with international students, talking to them about their experiences of being a student in the UK. Think about how to approach this and how you would prepare for these interviews. If you are not an international student, how much do you know about their experiences? How would you go about finding out enough about their experiences before you start writing your interview schedule?

Skill builder review

This task is designed to encourage you to think about how you would go about gaining background information to help you as you prepare to collect data.

You could start by looking at existing literature in this area, but that might only give you a limited amount of information. After all, your university may be very different from the university where the existing literature was gathered. It is helpful to extend your scope more widely in the preparation of a task like this. Does your university have students from a very diverse range of countries, or are they mostly from a certain geographic area? Are there, for example, international student societies at your university? Are they focused on particular degree routes?

Let's think about how you might go about finding some background like this. Assuming that you don't know any international students, it might be best to start by having a chat with some and listening to them when you ask about their experiences. You might find that they resent being lumped together as 'international students'; after all, if you were at a university overseas along with someone from another foreign country, how would you feel about being lumped together as if your experiences were the same? Alternatively, you might find that being with other people who are sharing your experience of being at a foreign university rather helpful and comforting. Why did they choose to come here? Why not go to a university in their home country? Do they feel accepted, or do they feel marginalised?

By asking questions and listening to what they tell you, you may well avoid falling into asking questions that don't really get at the core of their experience. For example, I have always been totally in awe of international students who are studying in their second or possibly third language. I can barely order a cup of coffee in another language, let alone write a scholarly essay. But I had fellow students for whom English was not their first language, who thought that this was not really that big a deal. They learnt English from an early age and were aware that we tend not to have the same focus on foreign language learning in school that they do.

Thinking about preparation from more than a theoretical perspective can help you to create better materials that can gather richer data.

Assignments

1. You have been asked to design a study to look at children's play. You have been given a free hand to design this study, using whatever method of data-gathering you wish, and choosing the environment to do it in. What are you going to do? What age range are you going to look at?

Are you going to observe in a natural environment or are you going to control it in some way? Would you consider interviews as part of your design? Set out your design, with justification of why you have selected that particular approach.

Summary: what you have learned

This chapter has introduced you to some of the main data collection methods in qualitative research methods. You should now be aware of some of the strengths and weaknesses of the different data collection methods and different functions that they can fulfil.

You have read about how to prepare recorded data for analysis and have made your first attempt at this. You should be able to understand that qualitative data collection and preparation is systematic and rigorous.

By reading this chapter and completing the tasks within it, you should be ready to start learning about qualitative analysis.

Further reading

Howitt, D (2010) Introduction to Qualitative Methods in Psychology. Harlow: Prentice Hall.

A comprehensive and readable book covering qualitative methods, data collection and analysis.

Jefferson, G (2004) Glossary of Transcription Symbols with an Introduction, in Learner, G (ed) *Conversation Analysis: Studies From The First Generation*. Philadelphia: John Benjamins.

A good glossary of the main transcription symbols, by the academic who introduced them. This is also useful as it shows symbols that are no longer used, but that you may encounter when reading older articles.

Silverman, D (2009) *Doing Qualitative Research*. 3rd edition. London: Sage.

One of the outstanding texts on qualitative research, this book takes you through the process of data collection and analysis, as well as giving good arguments for and against different types of data.

Chapter 9

Qualitative data analysis

Learning outcomes

The purpose of this chapter is to introduce you to some of the types of qualitative analysis and how to carry them out.

By the end of this chapter you will be able to:

- *select the most suitable form of analysis;*
- *analyse your data;*
- *prepare your findings for writing up.*

Introduction

Now you have your data, you need to do something with it so that you can determine some findings from it. You may well look at the volume of data you have and feel rather daunted by it. Where on earth do you start? How do you show that your findings are valid? It is important to use the correct analytic method for your data, and usually you will have a method in mind as you design your data collection.

This chapter is going to take you briefly through some of the main methods, and while this is too short a book to go into exhaustive detail, you should hopefully be able to make a start, as well as determine the correct method for your own data in the future.

There are differences between qualitative and quantitative methods that go beyond whether or not the methods are numerical in nature. Many of these are philosophical and you don't really need to get to grips with them, but probably the most important is the concept of reflexivity.

Reflexivity

Reflexivity is the concept of the involvement of the researcher in the data. Wetherell (2001) summarises it as *the way that the researcher acts on the world and the world acts on the researcher, in a loop* (p17). From a reflexive position, the question should be asked as to whether human beings interpreting the acts and interaction of other human beings can ever be truly objective. While we should always strive for objectivity, we should also acknowledge that our own position may influence our analysis. Our own position is also likely to influence both the topic for examination and the method that we are going to use. For example, if you have a family member with a serious illness, you may well be likely to want to research in that area. If you feel that this experience has had a major impact on your wider family, then you may want to examine the quality of this experience by using a qualitative methodology. Equally, you may be interested in the effect of brain injury on cognitive ability and would therefore be likely to utilise a more quantitative methodology.

The common analytic framework

All three analytic methods that you will be reading about share a core analytic framework. The key to this is the systematic nature of the analysis. It can be broken down into the following stages.

- Familiarisation with the data.

- Initial coding: identification of features.

- Secondary coding: grouping or dividing of features into more meaningful categories.

- Definition of coded features.

- Validation of coded features: do these features illustrate something meaningful about the data? What do they display in relation to existing literature?

- Write-up of findings.

It would be wrong to assume that qualitative analysis is a linear process and that you move smoothly from one stage to the next in an uninterrupted progression. Instead, you will find that you move between the stages, sometimes going back to the previous stage. As the features emerge, you should be ensuring that you are systematically evaluating the data to determine that the feature illustrates something meaningful. What do your findings mean? How are they relevant? Remember that your analysis should *be* an analysis. One of the worst mistakes made in qualitative analysis is that there is no real analysis; instead, the data is described or summarised, without actually analysing it and evaluating the findings. Provided you keep in mind the question, 'Am I saying something about the data, not just repeating it?', you should avoid this pitfall.

Thematic analysis

Thematic analysis is probably the most accessible of all the analytic forms in qualitative methods. It is systematic and can be applied to a wide variety of data, including interview, focus group, observation or documentary data. The specific thematic analysis method that you will be reading about here is that set out by Braun and Clarke (2006). This method is easy to learn and is flexible enough for adapting to your data.

Thematic analysis is a systematic interpretation of your data, with six identifiable stages. These stages help you to ensure that you are carrying out a systematic analysis and not just cherry-picking the things that support the position you want to take. You should remember that the path through the six stages is not one-way; you can go back and forward through the stages as themes and features emerge.

Stage 1

First, you must make sure that you are familiar with your data, reading and rereading it. The transcription process will help you with this. As you transcribe, you will find that you are already spotting common themes, or things that jump out at you as important. It is useful to note these things down as you go; they will form the first, very sketchy foundation of your analysis.

Stage 2

With your familiarity with the data, you can now start to code it. You have already got some notes from Stage 1, so now you can start to build on these. Coding is the process of finding and defining features within the data. Remember that this is not a content analysis, so you are not counting how many times a word is used. Instead, you are looking for the common ideas or patterns that emerge. It is important that you work through all your data, and give equal scrutiny to everything. This stage may take several readings and at first you may feel that there is little to see. But as you reread, codes and patterns will start to emerge.

Task — Code the data below.

99 Chris – What do you think the causes of such discrimination that

100 you talked about are? (.) I don't know, for example, a

101 Romany can be easily refused a job

102 (1.2)

103 Carla – °Because to me°- (.) >what can I say< (.) >what are the

104 causes<? (0.2) right? (.) I think that everything

105 *happens because of them (.) because even they don't want*

106 *(.) they don't have the desire (0.4) I don't think that*

107 *they are accepting (.) so, they would like to (0.4) to*

108 *(.) so, >they don't really like to work< (.) so,*

109 *as far as I know, >they don't own land to cultivate, to*

110 *farm< and >when they were offered a place to stay or*

111 *something like that< (.) I saw it on televi[sion (.)*

112 *Chris – [uh huh*

113 *Carla – They've put their horses in (.) so (.) >even if there*

114 *were flats< (.) where they managed to or (0.4) so*

115 *(0.4) even them, what they receive, they ruin (.)*

116 *so, they don't (0.8) °they don't respect, that's the*

117 *thing° (.)*

118 *Chris – Hmm*

(Extract from Tileagă, 2005, p615)

What codes did you generate?

Stage 3

Once you have coded your data and you feel that there are no more codes to identify, you can start to look for themes – the commonalities between codes that bring them together. At this point, you might wonder just what a theme is. Braun and Clarke (2006) say that a theme *captures something important about the data in relation to the research question* (p82). This is key at this stage. Just because something comes up a lot does not necessarily mean that it is important. This is where the need for interpretation comes in. You might be reading four interviews, but the possible theme only appears in one interview. Does that mean that you cannot use it? No, if it illustrates something important, of course you can use it. This stage is possibly the most challenging, and the most time-consuming, but this is the stage where the themes that you will be writing about really start to come together.

Stage 4

You can now start to review your themes, drawing them together to try to form more coherent findings. You will need to go back to your original data. Does your data support your themes? Is there enough data to justify a theme? Sometimes, you may find a really interesting theme, but when you go back to the original data, it shows itself to be a single incident and not reflective of the wider data set. As you review your themes, you may well find that some can be grouped together under a single umbrella theme. Alternatively, you may find that your themes can be broken down into several subthemes, each giving you a slightly different angle on your meta-theme. Don't be disappointed if some themes fizzle out as you review them. You'll find that others come along to take their place.

You are likely to find yourself going backwards and forwards in Stages 2, 3 and 4. This is fine; in fact, it is desirable. Howitt (2010) says that this back-and-forth process is desirable and can help to improve your overall analysis.

Stage 5

Now you need to clarify what your themes are, to give them names and to finalise what they are. These defined themes are going to be the basis of your report, so this is an important stage. You need to ensure that the themes are conceptually discrete, that they illustrate data in a meaningful way and are not simply collections of loosely related quotes. It is also important that you are able to identify what it is about your themes that is interesting and what they display in the data. Braun and Clarke (2006) warn against simply paraphrasing the content of your themes as you define them. They also give a particularly good tip: can you *describe the scope and content of your theme in a couple of sentences*? If you can't, then you need to go back and put in more work on your definitions. If you are confident about your themes, their content and what they illustrate, then you will write a much better report than if you are uncertain about them.

Stage 6

You have done the hard work now and you can write your report. As you do so, you will want to illustrate your work with examples from the data. Select the example that best encompasses the theme; don't try to put everything in. Remember that your report should do more than provide a commentary on what was said – it should be an analysis and should synthesise your findings with the existing literature, just as you would in a quantitative report.

Dealing with observation data

Observation data may look rather difficult to analyse, but it does lend itself to thematic analysis, if you take a rather lateral view of it. Think of it as a data set that details the environment and participants' actions in the same way that a transcript details what was said. One of the most important things with observation data is that you cannot infer internal motivations; you can only discuss the data as you see it. This can be difficult; we try to find explanations for behaviour as a normal part of our day-to-day lives. What we can say is that someone's behaviour is typical of something; laughing or crying are obvious behaviours, but try not to start looking at things like body language or other things that are too subjective. Just as with language data, as you read your field notes back, you can start to determine patterns of behaviour. From here, you can treat the analysis much as you do language data, going through the same processes.

Discourse analysis

Discourse analysis is the study of talk and interaction and seeks to examine how discourse achieves actions, and the power and persuasion of language. This is a succinct definition of discourse analysis, but to try to teach you how to actually do discourse analysis in such a short space of time would be almost impossible. Wooffitt (2005) says that *it is hard to capture in a formal guide what is essentially a series of interpretive engagements with data* (p42). Discourse analysis has been described by many of its practitioners as a 'craft skill', that is to say, you learn it by doing it. You could read a book on being a pilot, but would you then be able to fly a plane? Probably not, but it would give you a grounding in some of the things that you need to practise before you can fly that plane. In order to carry out competent discourse analysis, it is important that you have gained an understanding of the discipline of discourse analysis and discursive psychology. There are a number of different approaches to discourse analysis, but the one that you will be reading about here is that exemplified by practitioners at Loughborough University (Billig, 1991; Antaki and Widdicombe, 1998; Edwards, 1997; Edwards and Potter, 1992; Potter, 1996; Potter and Wetherell, 1987). By reading journal articles that utilise this method, you will start to see how the analysis works in practice across a range of applications. As your read more on discursive psychology, you will read about **discursive devices**. As I go through discursive devices with my students, they often tell me that they are fascinated by how often they encounter them in their day-to-day lives, as well as gaining an understanding of how those devices function in language. It would be a mistake to think that you can carry out discourse analysis by spotting devices. Instead, you may find that seeing some devices can alert you to something interesting, but they could also lead you to ignore other aspects of the transcript simply because they do not contain an easily identifiable device.

You will see that, in some ways, discourse analysis follows a similar path to thematic analysis. Just like thematic analysis, the analytic process of discourse analysis starts with an accurate transcript.

Also like thematic analysis, you are looking for patterns within the data, but the examination of the data should be informed by the core concepts of discourse analysis; that language is performative and that language is constitutive. Discourse analysis examines language as more than words in isolation; instead, it looks at language in its context and what that language achieves.

Task — Let us return to some of the data that you looked at in the Task on pages 122–3.

108 (.) so, >they don't really like to work< (.) so,

109 as far as I know, >they don't own land to cultivate, to

110 farm< and >when they were offered a place to stay or

111 something like that< (.) I saw it on televi[sion (.)

What do you think Carla achieves through this passage?

In the data extract, Carla is moving the origin of her opinions away from herself. She first says *as far as I know* (line 109), and then *I saw it on television* (111). If she is challenged because her position appears to be prejudiced or because her opinions are groundless, she can argue that it is only because she doesn't know anything else, or because the information that she has gained from the television is incorrect.

Most discourse analysts would probably say that you learn by trying, failing and trying again. A rather pessimistic picture of the analytic process is provided by Potter and Wetherell (1987) who say that *often it is only after long hours struggling with data and many false starts that a systematic pattern emerges. False starts occur as patterns appear, excitement grows, only to find that the pattern postulated leaves too much unaccounted, or results in an equally large file of exceptions* (p168). However, as well as the patterns that go nowhere, patterns emerge that are fruitful and illuminating.

Potter and Wetherell state that the process of analysis consists of two principal phases; the first is searching for patterns, whether of similarity or difference, and examining *function and consequences* (1987, p168) of the language. The next phase is the attempt to form hypotheses around the findings from the first phase. So you are examining that data, searching for features that are performative, and then trying to determine what it actually is that they are doing in that time and place. As you become more practised in discourse analysis, it does become easier.

In common with the analytic framework set out earlier in this chapter, discourse analysis approaches data in a systematic manner, coding it to break down the corpus into a more manageable data set. While you are doing analysis, it is important to consider the feature you are examining in the context of the rest of the data. As you read the data, you need to think about what the language is doing at that time and in that context. If you try to break the data down into very small sections, it starts to lose the meaning that it has as a whole. You might think of discourse as being like a Monet painting; if you stand too close to it, it just looks like blobs of paint, but if you stand back and view it as a whole, the full picture emerges. Discourse analysis is a long and often challenging process, but it is also an exciting and insightful analytic form.

Grounded theory

Grounded theory is an approach to research that encourages an open mind to the data and that seeks to create a theory that is 'grounded' in the data, rather than trying to find a way to make the data fit an existing theory. While you are going to create a grounded theory, you should not worry that you are going to create some grand psychological theory. Instead, in grounded theory, your theory is simply one about the overall data and one that applies primarily to that data. In grounded theory, the data collection and analysis run almost side by side, with areas of importance raised in the data inspiring further data collection. Grounded theory is a broad method, originally devised by Glaser and Strauss (1967). Their original work was about dying patients in hospital and their awareness of their impending deaths. They argued that research should not be bound by the constraints of theory and that theory should emerge to explain experience by analysing the data. However, the two academics started to move apart in their ideas on how to carry out grounded theory, although they do share some core principles. As a novice in grounded theory, it would be unwise to get too caught up in the rivalry of the two approaches. The key to grounded theory is that the systematic analysis of data can produce a theory that is an explanation of the area that you are studying.

Data collection in grounded theory is not a fixed process, but is bound up with the analytic process. The initial stage is the determining of an area of interest, followed by the collection of data around that area. As the data is collected, initial codes are generated. By responding to what your participants tell you, you can seek further data from them around that area of interest. Charmaz (2008) has carried out grounded theory analysis with people who have medical conditions that give them chronic pain. In her interviews with these participants, she found a pattern that emerged was the participants' discussion of pain and time as a relationship. Responding to this, she went on to ask more participants about their experiences of pain and time. This theoretical sampling helps to build the data corpus and to crystallise the research goal. Charmaz argues that it is this flexibility and ability to respond to participants that makes grounded theory work so valuable. If you were to adhere to a strict end to data collection before analysis, grounded theorists would argue that you would be imposing your own boundaries on the participants' responses.

Analysis in grounded theory can be described as having several principles:

- comparison;

- coding;

- categorisation;

- memo writing.

Data analysis is described by grounded theory as a constant comparative process: what is this person saying; what do they say elsewhere that relates to this; what does another participant say? In a similar fashion to thematic analysis, you are looking for features that say something meaningful. There are different types of coding that you will carry out. Open coding relates to the initial coding process. Axial coding is the stage at which you start to expand your codes and relate your open codes together. As you gather your codes, you should be able to start to categorise them into groups that share some kind of familiar aspect. These categories of codes may grow as you compare them back to the data, or they may peter out. You may need to recode some parts of the data as the categories emerge. Memo writing is the process by which you sketch out your idea of links between codes and categories, and the significance you feel that they have to your emerging theory. In a similar fashion to thematic analysis, you will be looking for coded themes to eventually form a meta-theme. This meta-theme will be, in essence, your theory.

Although you will have probably done some background reading to determine your research area, in grounded theory it is only once the data has been analysed that the literature review should take place. The idea is that you should not allow your literature review to overly influence your analysis.

Critical thinking activity

Analysis or evaluation?

Critical thinking focus: analysing and evaluating

Key question: *Objective analysis or subjective interpretation?*

It will be obvious to you that there is something of a gulf between qualitative and quantitative data and the manner in which it is analysed. With much quantitative data, there is no need to interpret it; it is a clear and unassailable result that can be analysed using a conventional formula. Provided you have correctly recorded the quantitative data, entered it into SPSS without error and selected the correct analysis, you will always get the same result. With qualitative analysis, the process is, by its very nature, more subjective. If you were to give everyone in a methods group a transcript and ask them to analyse it using a given qualitative method, each analysis would be different from the others. Some may have subtle differences and some differences may be much greater. Does this mean that one analysis is right and another wrong?

Consider the following questions to aid your critical appraisal.

Should only exact numerical analysis have value?

Provided the researcher makes their position explicit in the research, does the potential subjectivity of the qualitative methods detract from the value of the research?

Critical thinking review

This activity aims to help you understand the role of both qualitative and quantitative methods as part of the analytic toolbox, and that they each have their own valuable role in psychology research. As you have already learned, there is no single method to study every aspect of human behaviour and experience. In this activity, you may have argued about the concepts of validity and reliability, and how each of the approaches may fulfil one part to a greater extent than the other. You may also have thought about the necessity or value of proof rather than a 'snapshot' examination of a small participant pool. Obviously, for some things, the absolute objectivity of statistics is more important, while a more fine-grained examination may be more important in other cases.

Skill builder activity

Choosing a qualitative analytic method

Transferable skill focus: understanding and using data

Key question: *How do you go about choosing your qualitative analytic method?*

You have been presented with a data set that is made up of interactions on an internet site that functions as a support group for parents with children who have severe physical disabilities. Which of the qualitative analytic methods would you use to examine this data? Explain your choice of method and the features that you think would be most relevant in the data.

Skill builder review

You could, potentially, choose any of the three analytic methods to examine the data set described above. By doing this activity, it is important to think about how each of the three methods approaches language data. Each of the three methods would also be seeking different features from the data, and by understanding this it will help you in gaining skills in the methods.

Assignments

1. Critically evaluate two of the three methods from this chapter, evaluating the strengths and weaknesses of each. Illustrate your answer by using the data extract given in the Task on pages 122–3.

2. At the start of this chapter you were introduced to the concept of reflexivity and the idea that the researcher's position may influence both the topic of research and the interpretation of the data. Evaluate the role of the researcher in their research and whether the personal is necessarily a negative influence on the study.

Summary: what you have learned

In this chapter, you have been introduced to three of the main qualitative analytic methods. You have seen that there is a common analytic framework that will help you to plan your analysis. While it is difficult, if not impossible, to give a definitive and exhaustive guide as to how to carry out the methods in this chapter, you should have an understanding of how the methods are carried out.

Further reading

Antaki, C, Billig, M, Edwards, D and Potter, J (2003) Discourse Analysis Means Doing Analysis: A Critique Of Six Analytic Shortcomings, 1. *Discourse Analysis Online*. Available online at http://extra. shu.ac.uk/daol/current/

By understanding the common pitfalls of discourse analysis, it can really help you to understand what you should be doing. A highly recommended read.

Braun, V and Clarke, V (2006) Using Thematic Analysis in Psychology. *Qualitative Research in Psychology*, 3(2), 77–101.

This is a great why-to and how-to guide to thematic analysis, and probably the most comprehensive guide to the background and method of thematic analysis. Very highly recommended.

Dick, B (2005) *Grounded Theory: A Thumbnail Sketch*. [Online] Available at www.scu.edu.au/schools/ gcm/ar/arp/grounded.html

This gives background and method on grounded theory. Although designed for postgraduate students, it is very accessible and easy to read.

Chapter 10

Mixed methods

Learning outcomes

This chapter on mixed methods will focus on a rather obvious, yet relatively under-utilised, approach in research studies – the combination of both quantitative- and qualitative-based methods. It has been commented elsewhere that this represents a unique, separate research design – the so-called third major research approach (for example, Johnson et al., 2007; Tashakkori and Teddlie, 2003). However, in this book we have presented these two techniques separately and so perhaps it is unsurprising that many students think of them as entirely unrelated. This is not the case.

By the end of this chapter you should:

- *understand the concept of triangulation;*

- *have considered the benefits of this combined approach;*

- *be able to demonstrate the ability to design your own studies using mixed methods;*

- *have developed your reflective thinking skills;*

- *have exercised your independent learning skills.*

Introduction

Studies that have reported both qualitative and quantitative findings can be dated back to the early twentieth century, although an article by Campbell and Fiske (1959) was probably the first to document how this approach could be used to validate and strengthen research (see Johnson et al., 2007, for an overview). The frequency with which studies utilising both approaches are getting published is undoubtedly on the increase; there are now journals that cater specifically to the publication of research studies employing mixed methodologies (for example, *Journal of Mixed Methods Research* – 2007 to date). However, many students are simply not taught mixed methods at undergraduate level and may remain unaware of this approach.

So what exactly is meant by a mixed methods approach? Confusingly, different authors use a variety of terms to define what constitutes mixed methods. In the paper by Johnson et al. (2007), the authors invited colleagues from different academic institutions to provide their own definition of mixed methods research. While their definitions overlap on many points, some of the respondents disagreed about whether the mixed methods approach reflects a distinction between the methodological approach to framing a research study or is simply the combination of different methods and techniques in carrying out a research study.

The methodological interpretation of what constitutes mixed methods posits a combination of qualitative and quantitative approaches when first formulating a research question. Most textbooks, however, seemingly dictate that as a researcher you should choose a single method most appropriate to the research question. An issue here is that most researchers are wed to a particular approach. Certain types of research questions may simply be incompatible with the other approach (known as the **incompatibility thesis**); as an example, the majority of my published work uses functional and structural brain-imaging techniques to reveal differences relating to psychopathologies; no matter how innovative or insightful my questions, a semi-structured interview or thematic analysis of transcribed conversations will simply not deliver the metrics I need to obtain in this example. Researchers may have difficulty in framing the research question using any other approach due to a philosophical or epistemological barrier. This difficulty was crystallised during the **paradigm wars**.

The paradigm wars

It may sound silly now, but around 30 years ago a serious debate was raging in the field of research methods. Two schools of thought that opposed each other, perhaps unsurprisingly, were those who advocated quantitative methods and those who pursued a qualitative agenda. The arguments raged around the central tenets of how research ought to be conducted, and the debates veered towards the philosophies underlying the approaches of both camps. The quantitative position asserted that the study of the social sciences should be conducted in exactly the same format as the natural sciences, such as chemistry and physics. Consequently, the behaviour, cognition or opinion being studied should be viewed in exactly the same vein as phenomena studied in the physical sciences (Johnson and Onwuegbuzie, 2004, p14). This **positivist** stance (though see Moon and Moon, 2004) demanded that research be empirically based, i.e. objective, free from bias, and any conclusions be deduced from reliable, valid and demonstrable experimentation. Purists in the qualitative camp, however, argued that such objectivity and distancing of the self from the research was an artificial contrivance and had no wish to adopt such a style. They posited that it was not possible to disentangle oneself from the topic being studied (indeed, being subjective and informal was inevitable and indeed desirable), and attempting to demonstrate cause and effect conclusively was a fallacy. Instead, their **constructivist** viewpoint argued for an **inductive** approach, formulating theories and generalisations from specific observations – in effect, the polar opposite of the **deductive reasoning** underscoring the quantitative paradigm. Their data was 'richer', more intuitive and provided an immediacy that was simply not possible with the objective of quantifying and reducing complex processes and emotions into numerical indices. (For a more detailed analysis of the underlying philosophies of both approaches, see Further reading, page 141).

Task — Take a couple of minutes to refresh your understanding of the main advantages and disadvantages of employing these two approaches to research by completing Table 10.1.

Table 10.1: Pros and cons of the research approaches

Type of research	Advantages	Disadvantages
Quantitative	1.	1.
	2.	2.
	3.	3.
Qualitative	1.	1.
	2.	2.
	3.	3.

Thus the lines were drawn. As outlined in the basic arguments described in the previous paragraph, it would seem that these two approaches to research are quite simply incompatible. Take a look at the answers you wrote in Table 10.1 – the very advantages of one approach are related to the disadvantages of the other. It would seem they are the very antithesis of each other. Some authors have even suggested this might reflect a theoretical contempt for the other's ethos (see Giddings, 2006, for an exploration of this).

Why is this? Where has this disparity come from? Could it be unfamiliarity with the techniques used by the 'other side'? This is certainly a possibility – personally, I have publications in peer-reviewed journals dating back to 2003, but so far only one of these studies has used a qualitative approach. Perhaps this is due to the fact that my particular field of interest (psychopathology) is not really synonymous with qualitative methods – though as we will see, this need not be the case.

The outcome of the paradigm wars?

The paradigm wars of the 1980s have . . . turned to paradigm soup.

Buchanan and Bryman (2007, p486)

The outcome of the paradigm wars depends on which sources you choose to read. While there has been some further entrenchment of the more hardline positions, some authors (such as Howe,

1988) have been cited as stating that in an effort to end the wars and to help mixed methods gain equal status within both camps, the **pragmatist approach** has developed – akin to a phoenix rising from the flames (see Cameron and Miller, 2007).

Having read each of the chapters up to now, you are probably convinced that these approaches are diametrically opposed to each other; the type of research projects in which they are typically utilised seem to bear no resemblance to each other. You may not even have considered the possibility they *could* be reconciled into one study. However, if you think back to the previous chapters and the examples we have presented to illustrate both of these approaches, then you may begin to realise that it is unusual for a researcher to ask only a single research question. A research project is a collection of different studies, a detailed compilation of multiple research questions.

This is a big clue – even at a philosophical level, you can now probably discern that quantitative and qualitative designs can be used to answer different types of research questions on a given topic. This latter statement is the key to understanding how it is possible, and worthwhile, to use both types of paradigms to help uncover and learn more about any field of study.

Mixed methods

The rather more pragmatic definition of mixed methods loosely describes any study that utilises a combination of different methods (not philosophies). For instance, let's try to design a study to investigate the effects of a new caffeine drug designed to help students stay up late in order to complete those last-minute assignments. If we take a qualitative–quantitative approach, we might decide to undertake a feasibility study based on a single-case analysis of one participant before committing to recruit one group of participants in order to assess dose-related responses (tolerance levels) using a repeated-measures design. We may then go on to recruit several groups of participants in order to compare our drug with market rivals (substances currently used). By using a case study, we could examine how that participant responded to the drug and their experiences, and then use that quantitative approach to see if it could be extrapolated across a wider population. The qualitative findings could therefore inform our quantitative design.

From a different perspective, we might want to take a quantitative–qualitative approach. So we might look at the results of a repeated-measures design that examined participants' dose-related responses. We could then create a qualitative design that examined the experiences of participants, interviewing them about how they felt while using the drug and their perceptions of the quality of their study habits while using the drug. We could also recruit participants via social networking sites to provide diary data of their experiences of using the drug. By doing this, we could examine, in more depth, not just their ability to stay awake and therefore study longer, but also the impact of staying awake longer, and if they felt that their work improved or suffered by using the drug.

However, while these approaches are certainly valid, they are merely logical extensions of what you have been taught in previous chapters. They are examples of research in which the driving methodology is still one-dimensional; they continue to adhere to either a quantitative or qualitative framework and, as such, will not be discussed here. Instead, we will focus on combining quantitative and qualitative designs into a single research project. It may help to think of this approach as a 'multi-methods' research design instead, although we shall stick with the conventional title of 'mixed methods'. What we now need to uncover is how to harness the strengths of both approaches. We have discussed how they appear to be unrelated, but instead we can now portray these strengths as the flipside of a coin, viewing them as complementary. If we see the two methodological schools as opposing, we will inevitably lose benefits that can be gained from a truly mixed method approach. By acknowledging the need for recognition of the symbiotic relationship that quantitative and qualitative methods can enjoy, there is the potential to have a methodological approach that is greater than the sum of its parts.

What form do mixed methods studies take?

The literature on mixed methods will quite often portray the potential balance of qualitative and quantitative methods. You may see authors use terms such as QUAL > QUANT to denote the appropriate balance of the two approaches that could be used in a study. Studies may use both approaches either simultaneously in a parallel fashion, or in a linear sequential order (Morse, 1991). The mapping in Table 10.2 (based on Johnson and Onwuegbuzie, 2004) is an elegant précis of this distinction. Each numbered design in the third column indicates a mixed methodological approach, with the exception of 1 and 8, which maintain the ethos of purist qualitative and quantitative designs. As can be seen, it is possible to have studies that are either purely qualitative or purely quantitative in nature at the extremes of this scale (1 and 8). Moving inwards, there begins to be a gradual slide away from one approach dominating the style of research to what may be considered as more of an eclectic mix. This pattern continues until they both converge in the middle and arguably share equal status (4 and 5). As an example of this, let's consider a research project that explores the themes expressed during interviews with people regarding their views on law and order given the recent demonstrations against the Government's financial austerity policies. This, undoubtedly, has qualitative research objectives in its design, but suppose the researcher went on to conduct a content analysis of all the transcripts, identifying and logging the frequency of key phrases and words from particular social strata in response to certain questions asked during the interview? Such an analysis (2) would then bring a flavour of quantitative methods to the study and potentially uncover additional findings that otherwise would have remained unidentified.

Table 10.2: *Outline of possible mixed-methods designs*

Initial objective	Type of data collected	Type of analysis conducted
Qualitative	Qualitative	1. Qualitative
		2. Quantitative
	Quantitative	3. Qualitative
		4. Quantitative
Quantitative	Qualitative	5. Qualitative
		6. Quantitative
	Quantitative	7. Qualitative
		8. Quantitative

What might be the purpose of mixed methods?

So, using mixed methods might help to uncover findings and interpretation that otherwise might escape us. We can think of the mixed methods approach to be a holistic device used to ascertain a further level of detail and explanation, or to *give a rounded understanding of process and outcome* (Bazeley, 1999, p284). Put simply, there are at least five ways in which we might use mixed methods to enhance our research (Greene et al., 1989).

1. Triangulation

Triangulation can be (broadly) defined as *the combination of methodologies in the study of the same phenomenon* (Denzin, 1978, p291). The central argument is that by employing multiple methods, by virtue of basic geometry the combination of multiple viewpoints (findings) will facilitate a greater accuracy in studying phenomena. There is a general sense of convergence, agreement and corroboration of the interpretation, stemming directly from the results obtained via these the disparate methods.

2. Complementarity

Complementarity is an extension of triangulation used to clarify or elaborate findings derived from one method with those results derived from an alternative method. This term stems from a principle of physics, which suggests that a complete description of any phenomena necessitates the use of two distinct theories to complement each other; by treating these two types of data as separate, they complement and enhance the interpretability and significance of results obtained.

3. Development

A third purpose of mixed methods is to use the results from the qualitative approach to help develop or inform the quantitative method (and vice versa). For instance, suppose you wished to (quantitatively) measure the impact on family life of living with someone who had a diagnosis of autism. There is not a questionnaire that you could simply pick up off the shelf and use, so instead you may need to design one yourself. In order to know what questions might be most beneficial, you might consider interviewing a couple of such families during the planning stage. This qualitative approach may then guide you in selecting and generating appropriate items for this new quantitative measure that will be used to answer the original research question.

4. Initiation

Similarly, **initiation** is a process in which the seemingly contradictory results of one method are used as a basis to question and reformulate the approach of the other. The incongruent findings create a paradoxical situation, which, rather than muddying the waters, can be seen as an opportunity to make new hypotheses and rethink research questions to uncover the source of this disequilibrium.

5. Expansion

Expansion can be viewed in a similar vein to elaboration. Its intended purpose is to extend the range of enquiry by virtue of employing different methods required as necessary when investigating different aspects of the research question. Simply by using multiple methods, the scope of the enquiry is expanded; thus new results outside of those first considered may, potentially at least, now be obtained.

Task — *Theory of nasty mind* (Happé and Frith, 1996) describes the intact but skewed theory of mind in particular individuals. The standard false-belief tasks typically used to measure theory of mind (such as the Sally-Ann dolls) are usually passed or failed and cannot measure any qualitative differences in responses. If you wished to conduct similar research, how might you use a mixed methods approach to facilitate this?

The best of both worlds?

The consensus among many textbooks on research methods seems to be an implicit assumption that the disadvantages of both the qualitative and quantitative approaches are somehow neutralised or eclipsed by the advantages gained when combining both types in a mixed methods approach (Greene and Caracelli, 1997). But what is the evidence for this? Is it always the case that mixed methods is an advantageous approach? Could this be a case of the emperor's new clothes? We have previously discussed how research method modules often teach qualitative and quantitative approaches separately. There may be some passing acknowledgement of a relation to the overarching concept of 'research methods', but in practice they are taught separately. Furthermore, the staff members who make up the respective teaching groups usually follow this same separation; most staff in psychology departments will adopt one or the other approach but very rarely employ mixed methods themselves. Giddings (2006) argues that this dichotomy is contributing to the *methodological talking past each other phenomenon* (p200).

There is an element of paying lip service to the concept of mixed methods (yes in theory, no in practice), despite many research books advocating the benefits of mixed methods approaches. There is also the potential problem that most psychologists are trained in their particular method, and that they cannot really engage in truly mixed methods unless they have had specific training in synthesising different methods. The possible pragmatic issues of mixed methods are also a challenge; not every area of study would lend itself to mixed methods. To try to force mixed methods to be dominant would be just as dogmatic as the approach of those methodologists who claim that only their method is truly worthwhile.

Giddings (2006) argues further that even for those who follow a pragmatic approach, the issues surrounding the efficacy of mixed methods research may appear straightforward and uncomplicated. The cry of 'Let's just get on with it' may very well be the calling card of a pragmatist researcher, but Giddings suggests that qualitative researchers may have mixed feelings about the rather superficial way in which mixed methods researchers are using qualitative methods. Equally, quantitative researchers may harbour some discontent with the proliferation of mixed methods studies, which arguably require less specific methodological expertise at the expense of producing more generalisable and more intuitive interpretations of results.

Critical thinking activity

Incompatibility of methods

Critical thinking focus: reflection

Key question: Can opposing research methodologies be juxtaposed?

Inspect the following three pairs of antonyms. They are descriptions typically associated with quantitative and qualitative methods respectively.

1. Deductive versus inductive.

2. Confirmatory versus exploratory.

3. Empirical versus subjective.

How can these approaches be juxtaposed in a spirit of cooperative enquiry when they appear to come from diametrically opposed ethoses?

Critical thinking review

This activity is designed to have you reflect on the apparent incompatibility of quantitative and qualitative research methods. This is no trifling matter – a war was raged in academia over this! The use of antonyms reinforces the apparent schisms that existed between these two approaches – or do they? Might the very fact these methods differ so much actually prove to be a strength rather than a weakness in their combined usage?

Skill builder activity

Design your own mixed methods study

Transferable skill focus: independent learning

Key question: *How easily can research questions be tackled with a mixed design approach?*

Ketamine is a drug that, at the appropriate dosage, can mimic certain symptoms of schizophrenia (for example, paranoia, dissociation). It is often used in medical research for this very purpose. You have been asked to design a study to assess the acute effects of administering this drug to healthy participants.

Design the study with these questions in mind.

How can you accurately assess the effects of acute administration of the drug?

Will standard questionnaires and visual analogue scales capture the subjective feelings being experienced?

How can you incorporate the appropriate methods to facilitate the processes of triangulation, complementarity, development, initiation and expansion?

Skill builder review

This task is one faced by many researchers attempting to incorporate a mixed methods approach into their work. In attempting to accommodate the processes of triangulation, complementarity, development, initiation and expansion, the design needs to have these approaches dovetail together in a seamless integration and not feel shoehorned, i.e. forced together merely for the sake of it.

Practising this type of activity helps develop your independent thinking and your critical, creative and organisational skills in relation to the design and creation of psychological experiments. In order to utilise a mixed methods approach, care must be taken to consider how these methods may be implemented in order to assist you in the research process. They are merely tools to be used at your convenience to demonstrate new knowledge in psychological fields of study, but used incorrectly they will not yield any useful information.

Assignments

1. Many research methods courses and books present quantitative and qualitative approaches to research as though they are separate and distinct subjects. There may be some passing acknowledgement of a relation to the overarching concept of 'research methods', but in practice they are taught separately. What is your opinion on this apparent divide? Do you consider this to be an appropriate or deleterious approach to research methods teaching? Why?

2. As previously mentioned, in some literature there appears to be an automatic assumption that the combination of qualitative and quantitative methods in research will always have a positive outcome. Is this assumption correct? Are the criticisms of this assumption merely based on turf protectionism?

Summary: what you have learned

This chapter has introduced you to the concept of using mixed methods in the attempt to answer research questions. We described how mixed methods can refer not only to an epistemological or philosophical approach to enquiry, but more specifically to using a combination of different approaches and methods to study a phenomena. In particular, we focused on the combination of qualitative and quantitative research methods in a single study, and how they may enhance research through the processes of triangulation, complementarity, development, initiation and expansion.

Social science has often been labelled a 'soft' science – trying to emulate the principles of study in the conventional 'hard' sciences, such as physics and chemistry. I once read a talkback comment posted on the www.BadScience.net website following a debate on 'The glorious mess of real scientific results' and liked it so much that I paraphrase it for use in my lectures: the thrust of the argument was that social science, with its multiple layers of complexity (organisms, free will, biases, social behaviour and so forth), is actually a harder science to study than simply working with chemicals or physical forces. Due to this complexity, it has been argued that different methodological approaches are *required* in order to comprehend the many factors involved in the phenomena studied in social sciences (Greene and Caracelli, 1997).

Further reading

Giddings, LS (2006) Mixed-methods Research: Positivism Dressed in Drag? *Journal of Research in Nursing*, 11(3), 195–203.

This is an easily digestible paper that provides a critique on the assumption that mixed methods research is always an advantageous strategy.

Greene, JC, Caracelli, VJ and Graham, WF (1989) Toward a Conceptual Framework for Mixed-Method Evaluation Designs. *Educational Evaluation and Policy Analysis*, 11(3), 255–274.

This paper gives a good account of the advantages of using a mixed methods approach to research.

Johnson, RB and Onwuegbuzie, AJ (2004) Mixed Methods Research: A Research Paradigm Whose Time Has Come. *Educational Researcher*, 33(7), 14–26.

This article is a succinct description of the philosophical and epistemological differences between qualitative and quantitative research methods approaches.

Johnson, RB, Onwuegbuzie, AJ and Turner, LA (2007) Toward a Definition of Mixed Methods Research. *Journal of Mixed Methods Research*, 1(2) 112–133.

This paper will brief you on the historical account of the rise of the mixed methods approach, past and current definitions of what this actually means, and discussions from various researchers as to how they understand what this approach entails.

Chapter 11

Common problems

Learning outcomes

This chapter will cover some of the main problems encountered when conducting research. It will offer possible solutions to the outlined problems while highlighting a cautious approach.

By the end of this chapter you should:

- be aware of methods of dealing with missing data and the possible consequences thereof;

- understand the need for the identification and examination of outliers;

- appreciate how and when ordinal data can be used as interval data;

- understand the relevance of parametric assumptions;

- know the importance of type I and II errors in relation to statistical test outcomes.

Problems in the collection of data

The collection of data can, in itself, be problematic, either within a laboratory setting or a questionnaire design. In the laboratory setting, participants may give erroneous measures (those which make up the dependent variable) through a variety of factors (distractions, not reading the instructions clearly etc.). With the increasing use of computer-based experiments, these effects may not come to light until after the experiment. The resultant data may not be truly representative of the actual experimental condition. Of course, in reality, you could never expect perfect data (indeed, if the data looks too perfect you should be suspicious). However, if there were a large influence upon the data, the overall calculation or score (dependent variable) would be totally different to reality. In such instances, calculation of the mean score and the resultant standard deviation for the overall condition upon which **parametric tests** derive population parameters would also be in error. The question therefore remains: how do we spot this and what do we do? We will deal with this question a little later when we look at **outliers** and the distribution of data (see the sections on parametric assumptions on page 147 and parametric preference on page 152).

Similar problems also apply to questionnaire designs. Questions may be answered incorrectly. If the overall score is dependent upon the summation of the results of a questionnaire, the effect upon the overall score may be substantial and, again, influence the overall mean and standard deviation of the data, thereby influencing whether there is a statistical difference between the conditions (or not). This can be minimised within the design stage of a questionnaire by making sure there are a sufficient number of questions that tap the construct under question so that the inclusion of erroneous data has minimal impact (see Chapter 1). In addition, this is further minimised as you increase the number of participants. Problems may arise and be more trouble-some when data is missing – for example, if answers to certain questions within a questionnaire measuring a dimension of interest are missing. On the face of it, the simplest solution in this case would be to recruit another participant to make up for the missing data. Alternatively, you could simply remove this participant from the analysis (we will return to this point later on). To do so without thought and justification could, arguably, be defined as 'massaging the data', or worse, as 'fraudulent', an accusation a good researcher would never want to face. It is vitally important to take a step back and ascertain if there was any reason for the missing data (is it just with this participant's data set or is this found consistently with other participants?) Whatever your method of data collection, you can never just discard data unless you have good, sound, arguable reasons to do so.

Missing data

The impact of missing data is not purely dependent upon the amount, but also the pattern of data loss. If the missing data is random, then there is less of a problem. If the missing data is truly random, representing less than five per cent of a large data set, then any method of adjusting for the missing data will result in a similar outcome (Tabachnick and Fidell, 2001). Of course, the problem is defining what constitutes a large data set. So we can never truly be certain to what extent missing data affects our overall conclusion. However, you should never assume that missing data is random. It needs careful examination. Is the missing data highly correlated with a particular experimental condition? In addition, demographic and participant profile data needs to be examined (and should always be recorded as a matter of course). For example, it may be that participants of a particular age, gender, ethnicity, socioeconomic status or even occupation may be highly correlated with the omission of a particular question. This can be examined by setting up a pretend variable that categorises those participants with missing and non-missing data. The next stage is to conduct appropriate tests of mean difference (for example, t-tests) where you ascribe the dependent variable as one of the other measures (for example, age, income, etc.) If there are no statistically significant differences between the measures, then how you deal with missing data becomes less critical. If, however, there is a significant difference, with large dif-ferences in effect size, then how you deal with missing data becomes more important (Tabachnick and Fidell, 2001). The examination of missing data may allude to hitherto psychologically interesting characteristics and require further investigation. However, this may not be helpful in the predicament in which we find ourselves. What are the options available to us? There are two broad options available: deletion or substitution. As a rule of thumb, if the data loss on any dimension, or part thereof, which constitutes the dependent variable is more than five per cent, then it is highly questionable that anything should be done to the data other than gathering more through further recruitment of participants. It is important to note that there is no perfect solution to missing data (Clark-Carter, 2010). Often, it is a question of explicitly stating within the results section of the research report (or paper) what has been done so that your decisions are transparent to those who read the research presented.

Deletion of participant data

The most common way to remove data is either through list-wise or pair-wise deletion. In the case of list-wise deletion, only participants who have provided all the data required from them will be used in the analysis. This form of deletion is the most severe in the reduction of your sample size. Although some authors suggest this is too severe and at times unnecessary (Pallant, 2010), caution should be used with the less severe alternative – pair-wise deletion.

In the case of pair-wise deletion, as much data as possible is used and data is only excluded if it is missing from a specific analysis. However, as Clark-Carter (2010) points out, there are instances when such an approach leads to differences in samples sizes inclusion for specific sets of analyses in which the final inferential statistic derived may come from different sets of participant data – for example, tests of co-linearity prior to a regression analysis.

Substitution of missing data

In the case of missing data, the alternative to its removal is its replacement with a representative data point (imputation). The most common approaches to this are:

- mean value substitution;

- median value substitution;

- substitution through regression analysis;

- expectation minimisation;

- multiple imputation.

In the method of mean substitution, the data already obtained for a particular variable (or condition) is used to calculate a mean value, which is then substituted for the missing value. The advantage of this method is that the overall mean is not altered, but can have a considerable effect upon the variance. The resultant reduction of variance can lead to a considerable over-estimation of a difference between two conditions. For this reason, some authors (for example, Pallant, 2010) suggest that this method should never be used. Of course, the extent to which the variance is affected by this approach is dependent upon the extent to which data is missing.

Median substitution is the substitution of the median value instead of the mean value. Arguably, there is little difference, other than being less affected by severe data points within the data set.

Regression analysis can be used as a more objective measure for data substitution if other variable(s) can be used as predictor (independent) variable(s). In this case, a regression analysis can be conducted in order to use the regression equation to calculate the value of the missing variable. Once again, the substituted value may deviate less than what would be expected in reality, with the consequent reduction in the variance. This would result in the overestimation of the inferential statistics metric (t-value, F value, etc.)

Expectation minimisation is where the missing data point is repeatedly estimated until the estimated value remains more or less constant with each new estimation attempt. This is an iterative process in which, initially, the means, variances and co-variances are estimated for the data present and are used to estimate the missing values. These estimated values are then used subsequently to re-estimate the substituted values, which then are used in the next re-estimation of values (and so on). The values are obtained through procedures that estimate the regression equations that relate all variables to each other. Of course, the same problem arises, in that the distribution around the mean diminishes, possibly leading to a greater estimation of difference. However, modern statistical software packages (for example, SPSS) introduce some error following a pattern of normal distribution in the estimation process in order to counter this problem.

Multiple imputation involves the creation of multiple data sets from the original data set with its missing values. These new multiple 'complete' sets are each used, in turn, to conduct the typical statistical test related to the research question. The mean parameter estimate for the statistical tests can then be used. This technique allows for a critical evaluation of the results obtained as the variability of parameter estimates can be examined in relation to the different estimated data sets.

Whichever option is used in relation to missing data, caution must always be applied to the interpretation of results. Therefore, it is important to examine the effect of any data manipulation upon the recorded data. This can be done quite simply by comparing the results obtained with the missing-data data set with that of the modified set. It is more important to note the difference in any effect size measurement rather than the statistical significance, as the change in statistical significance may be purely due to differences in sample size. However, if there is a large difference in the effect sizes produced, then further caution should be applied to any explicit interpretation of findings.

Preparing the data for analysis

Most analysis conducted now uses some form of spreadsheet format whereby all the data collected is entered prior to the statistical analysis. Even at this stage of data input, you should critically examine the data. There is a tendency, especially when using data from computer-based experiments in which each participant undertakes a number of trials, to merely use the mean or median value for a particular condition without paying too much attention to the raw data used in its calculation. Within certain psychology experiments, it is not uncommon for researchers to delete the first few trials of data, as the level of performance tends to improve rapidly, reflecting the participant getting used to the task requirements. This noisy data is often merely reflective of task uncertainty, but it could be argued that, to some extent, it also relates to task learning. Alternatively, some researchers present participants with practice trials. Whatever method you use, it needs to be explicitly stated in the research write-up. However, there are times when, for some inexplicable reason, the data obtained for a participant seems very odd when compared with that of the other participants – an outlier. The presence of such a data point needs to be investigated. Is it an error in data entry (incorrect transcription of data), or possibly some part of the experiment that did not function properly? Is it possible that a bug within the program has resulted in the erroneous recording of data? Whatever the reason, any odd data point needs to be investigated thoroughly to explain its presence. If it is obvious that this data point was clearly not representative due to some external error, it can be safely removed (for example, the participant developed a migraine or was distracted during the experimental session). This issue of outliers, their definition and their removal (or adjustment) can be understood in relation to the underlying assumption of normal distribution fundamental to parametric tests.

Outliers

Whenever we take a sample (from the population) and we assume that the scores within a population are normally distributed, we expect our data to reflect this, too. However, in practice, it is possible that aberrant or extreme values may enter our data set. This may be due to two different factors. The first is quite simply a result of measurement (or transcription) error. The second is that the data may be representative of two different populations within one sample. There are numerous methods for the identification of a possible outlier. For example, software programs such as SPSS allow outlier identification through their box plot function in which outliers are easy to identify as they are labelled in relation to the dataset. Alternatively, you can identify outliers based upon the logic of the normal distribution curve in which an outlier is labelled as any data point within a sample that is three or more standard deviations (in both directions) away from the mean. Taking this in the context of the normal distribution curve (see Figure 11.1 on page 150), this represents data that is so extreme as to represent a 0.26 per cent likelihood of happening by chance. As a rule of thumb, this is a good metric to which to adhere. However, it also important to examine the potential outlier graphically in relation to all the data collected. This can be done either through a histogram or scatterplot. In this way, you can make an informed decision as to whether the unusual data truly belongs (theoretically) to the data set collected.

There is often a desire to remove outliers merely on the basis of their value rather than any valid methodological reason. The extent to which removal of outliers will affect sample mean and standard deviation will, of course, be moderated by the extremity of the value and overall sample size. Therefore, if there is no definitive reason on methodological grounds to remove these data points, then they should not be removed.

The parametric assumptions

Parametric tests require certain criteria to be fulfilled before they can be used. These are typically:

- level of data (either interval or ratio);

- independence;

- homogeneity of variance (between-participants tests);

- normal distribution.

Of course, there may be others dependent upon the actual inferential test used (for example, sphericity for a within-participants analysis of variance – ANOVA).

Interval or ratio data

It is often explicitly stated that in order to conduct parametric tests, the only type of data that can be used is interval or ratio. However, there are instances when we can (and often do) use ordinal or rank data, typically in questionnaires. Indeed, a large proportion of psychological research uses questionnaires. Typically, an item will ask a question (or make a statement) and the participant has to indicate their response on a Likert (1932), or similar, scale. The example on page 148 is part of a questionnaire designed to provide a measure of social phobia. (Note that it does not measure social phobia directly.)

Q. I am easily embarrassed in social situations.

Strongly disagree	Disagree	Slightly disagree	Neither agree/ disagree	Slightly agree	Agree	Strongly agree
1	2	3	4	5	6	7

If there are seven or more levels within the measure (as shown above), then parametric tests can be used so long as all the other parametric assumptions have been fulfilled (Tabachnick and Fidell, 2001). However, this should not result in the deliberate expansion of the levels within a question to fulfil this criterion. Let us return to the following question from the Skill builder activity in Chapter 3 (see page 44).

Q. To what extent do you agree with the statement: 'Statistics is my life'?

Strongly agree	Quite strongly agree	Agree	Mostly agree	Agree a little	Neutral	Disagree a little	Mostly disagree	Disagree	Quite strongly disagree	Strongly disagree
1	2	3	4	5	6	7	8	9	10	11

In this case, the assumptions for parametric inclusion have been fulfilled, but in so doing, the scale has rendered the answers useless and reflective of poor methodology. However, as is often the case with most questionnaires, collection of data questions is combined and summated – indicative of an attempt to fully capture the dimension in question (see Chapter 2) while at the same time fulfilling parametric requirements.

Returning to the question on social phobia, it is important to note that the different categories on the seven-point scale (strongly disagree to strongly agree) are assigned a numerical value, which serves to reinforce the fact that categories are worth more or less than others. We might expect people with social phobia to score highly on this questionnaire and those without social phobia to score considerably lower. Now let's suppose two participants answered this particular item – one ticked the 'strongly disagree' category and the other 'agree'. On the basis of this, we may infer that the latter participant has a higher level of social phobia due to their score (6 versus 1), but we cannot determine how much more socially phobic they are in real life. The score can differentiate the categories according to a rank order, but this difference gives no indication as to the magnitude of the true difference in their degree of social phobia. Although the difference between disagree and strongly disagree may appear to be worth one point ($2 - 1 = 1$), as outlined previously there is no way to ascertain if this categorical one-point difference is the same as the one-point difference between the 'slightly agree' and 'neither agree/disagree' categories ($5 - 4 = 1$). This is an important fact to keep in mind.

Independence of data

This is merely the expectation that the data (or observation) from each participant is independent and is not influenced by external factors – for example, that a self-reported score is not being influenced by other participants.

Homogeneity of variance

This is where there is an expectation that the variability of scores (variance) around the mean between the conditions is comparable. Caution should be applied to those statistical tests that test for assumptions of variance as they often utilise the same assumptions as parametric tests. If the sample size is small, they might indicate that there is a problem when indeed there is none, and vice versa – with large sample sizes, a small violation may be indicated as problematic (Clark-Carter, 2010). Therefore, for example, in the case of a between-participants t-test, with equal sample sizes, a good rule of thumb for **homogeneity of variance** is to multiply the smallest variance (sd^2) by a factor of four, which should be equal to, or exceed, the value of the largest variance. With unequal sample sizes, this should be reduced down to a factor of two (Clark-Carter, 2010). If heterogeneity of variance occurs then Welch's t-test should be used in preference (this is done automatically in SPSS). For a one-way between-participants ANOVA, the same rule applies in relation to homogeneity: a times four multiple for equal sample sizes across the groups reducing to a factor of two for unequal-sized groups (Clark-Carter, 2010). In the case of mixed multifactorial ANOVAs, issues of homogeneity of variance should be examined for the between-participant components with the same rules applied.

Normal distribution

This is the assumption that a set of data/scores/observations is normally distributed around a mean and that the further the values are away from the mean the less likely they are to occur.

Taking the normal distribution curve (**Gaussian distribution**), the area under the curve represents 100 per cent of the scores within a population. The y-axis indicates the frequency, and the x-axis the number of standard deviations the particular score is away from the mean. It is immediately apparent that the further away the data point is from the mean, the less likely its occurrence. For example, only 2.15 per cent of all scores are two or more standard deviations above the mean. So, if we have a mean of 100 (this is at 0 standard deviations) and a standard deviation of 10, then only 2.15 per cent of scores would be expected to have a value of 120 or more. Likewise, one standard deviation above the mean is representative of 34 per cent of the total population scores so it is expected that 34 per cent of the population would have a score between 100 and 110. Taking one

Figure 11.1: *Area under the normal distribution curve*

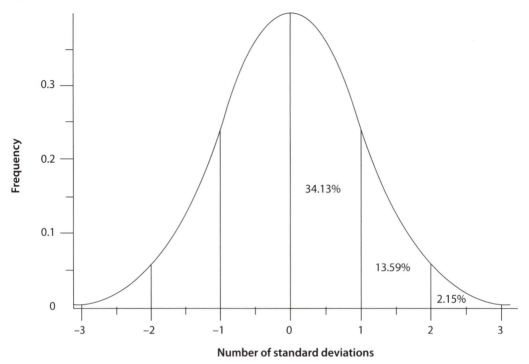

standard deviation each side of the mean, it would be expected that 68.26 per cent of the population would have a score between 90 and 110, and so on. By knowing how many standard deviations a score is away from the mean, the likelihood of that score occurring can be assessed. The number of standard deviations a score is away from the mean is calculated through z scores, in which z scores of 1, -1, 2, etc. denote the number of standard deviations a score is away from the mean. Conversion of a particular observed score into its z score (also called standard score) can be easily done through the following equation.

$$z = \frac{\text{observed score} - \text{sample mean}}{\text{standard deviation}}$$

Examination of normal distribution can be most easily undertaken through the use of histograms. Deviations from normal distribution are indicated by the level to which it is skewed. In such cases, the data can be either skewed to the left or to the right. Simply put, there is a lack of symmetry around the mean (a long tail to the left or right). The extent of this lack of symmetry can be ascertained using a skewness statistic. In the case of the SPSS program, which produces a skewness statistic (in the explore data option), a skewness value around ±1 should be considered sufficient as to warrant a breach of parametric assumption (Dancey and Reidy, 2007). However, whatever skewness measure is used, it should not be wholly relied upon as an absolute. Sample size can affect the accuracy of this statistic in which large samples are often deemed to violate assumptions of skewness more readily than smaller ones (Clark-Carter, 2010). Any investigation into non-normal distribution should also involve looking at the data itself. However, if the distribution is skewed, it may be possible to transform the data, dependent upon the nature of the non-normalised distribution or to utilise non-parametric tests instead. However, caution should be applied as it is often erroneously assumed that parametric tests are distribution free. These tests do not require normal distribution, but do require the distributions to be comparable between the conditions; as such, this needs to be taken into account.

Assumptions of sphericity

Within-participant parametric tests often stipulate the assumption of sphericity. This issue, more than others, can be problematic as some authors think that sphericity can never be assumed and others that, on the whole, it should be assumed. Students, unlike in any other area of psychology, assume that there is a clear, set-in-stone approach to statistical analysis. The problem is further complicated by the fact that you cannot rely totally on the tests for sphericity that are often used within common statistical packages. However, with a little careful examination, this issue can be resolved easily. Two main outcomes of analysis can be assured: either 'sphericity assumed', indicated by the non-adjusted output, or the 'violation of sphericity' as indicated by a Greenhouse-Geisser adjustment (this adjustment involves the degrees of freedom used in the F-value calculation of the ANOVA). If you examine the output of the adjusted and non-adjusted ANOVA and the significance level is the same, then you can assume sphericity. If the non-adjusted sphericity-assumed ANOVA is non-significant, you can be assured that the adjusted will also yield non-significance. The only time that there is a problem is if the non-adjusted (sphericity-assumed) yields statistical significance and the Greenhouse-Geisser yields non-significance. In this case, it is advisable to report both outcomes and discuss these contradictory findings in the context of the research. In so doing, there is a transparency of finding in which the reader can make an informed choice as to the outcome of the research.

The robustness of parametric tests

Often, when the parametric assumptions of a test have been violated (to a lesser or greater degree), there is a temptation to state the default defensive position that as parametric tests are robust and some parametric assumptions can be violated, the results of the parametric test are, de facto, valid. This is true up to a point. However, it is difficult at times to empirically quantify to what degree parametric tests can be violated. Therefore, when in doubt as to the seriousness of parametric assumption violation, it is advisable to undertake the non-parametric equivalent. If the outcomes of the non-parametric and parametric test of inference are close, there is a strong point for continuing to use the parametric test.

The parametric preference and error types

Whenever possible, it is advisable to conduct parametric tests rather than their non-parametric counterparts. One of the main reasons for this is that parametric tests are *usually* more statistically powerful in that they are less likely to fail to reject the null hypothesis when they, in fact, should reject the null hypothesis. This is related to the two different types of error possible within inferential statistics: type I and type II errors.

As mentioned before, *we never set out to prove the experimental hypothesis*, merely to reject the null hypothesis. We estimate the likelihood of the probability of the different conditions coming from the same set of scores if the null hypothesis is true (there is, in reality, no difference between the groups/conditions). Consider for a moment a group of 200 individuals who have been given a memory test. Their scores have been recorded on a piece of paper and put in a hat. If a sample of scores was taken randomly from the hat, say 35 scores, it would be expected that the mean and standard deviation calculated from that sample (the 35 bits of paper) would be close to, if not representative of, the mean and standard deviation of all the scores within the hat. If this process were repeated time and time again with the full set of 200 scores available, we would find that the means obtained would be, on the whole, quite close. However, there would be times when the difference between the means obtained would be unexpectedly large. In fact, all things being equal, the greater the difference between the means the less likely its occurrence. The way the data would be spread would be representative of a normal distribution (see Figure 11.1 on page 150) except that this would be a distribution of means (instead of individual scores) and instead of standard deviations, standard error would be used instead (standard error is merely standard deviations for means). What we do with inferential statistics is that we take samples from the population and infer the parameters from our sample to the population. If there is truly no difference between the experimental conditions, the manipulation has no effect; the means should not be too dissimilar. However, if the means are very different, we work out the likelihood of the means being different due to sampling error. If this is so unlikely as to be five per cent or less chance, then we reject the null hypothesis. This leads the researchers (and us) to elect the experimental hypothesis as the only credible alternative. However, setting this value at five per cent or less does mean that we are, of course, in danger of committing a type I error. The type I error is rejecting the null hypothesis when it is, in fact, true. The chance of making this error is, of course, five per cent. As we can never be absolutely certain that we have not made a type I error, this should emphasise the importance of replication of research. However, the other side of the coin is reflected by the likelihood of making a type II error – that is, failing to reject the null hypothesis when, in fact, it is false (in other words, failing to 'accept' the experimental hypothesis in preference to our null hypothesis). Unlike the probability of making a type I error, which is set at five per cent (we accept statistical significance at $p<0.05$ or less), the probability of making a type II error is affected by a number of factors: the effect size, number of participants, tail of the tests, the statistical test used and the level of statistical significance. A desirable level of **power** for statistical tests is 0.8 (Cohen, 1988) – representative of an 80 per cent chance of not making a type II error. This level of power is considered an appropriate level as raising the power above 0.8 would become increasingly expensive in the recruitment of additional participants.

Non-significance of results does not indicate poor design

Often students, especially dissertation students, incorrectly ascribe non-significance of their study as indicative of a poor piece of research. This, of course, may be due to bad conception of the research question or the use of inappropriate measures. However, this may not be the case. It may simply be that they did not have enough statistical power and therefore were highly likely to make a type II error – a failure to reject the null hypothesis when, in fact, it is false. Quite simply put, there were not enough participants. On occasions such as this, it is worthwhile conducting a retrospective power analysis. This requires the computation of the effect size appropriate to the parametric test conducted. Since the significance level we require is set at 0.05, it is simply a question of finding the appropriate table in a statistics book (for example, Clark-Carter, 2010) and looking up the sample size that would have produced a power of 0.8. Quite often, examination of statistical power related to the sample size and effect size results in an effect size estimate well below 0.8. For example, if the power was 0.5, then we are actually saying that the probability of making a type II error is no better than merely flipping a coin. Alternatively, there are now some easily available power analysis programs, such as G Power, that can do this calculation for you. It is therefore worthwhile on the non-significance finding to investigate the statistical power involved. In addition, it is always useful when designing any study to examine a related study and use its findings to ascertain how many participants would possibly be needed for your study in order to reach a power of 0.8.

Psychological reality versus statistical reality

An important distinction to make in the outcome of results is that of statistical significance and psychological significance. Too often the fact that there is a statistically significant difference between two conditions seems to override the importance of the magnitude (effect size and/or means) of the difference between the conditions or the psychological implications thereof. It is important to put findings in context and relate the implications of the findings practically within the area of research. This requires good understanding and utilisation of descriptive statistics and a thorough awareness of the flaws and strengths of the methodology used. The ultimate goal of the use of statistics is to make greater sense of complex information within its limits of certainty. A good understanding of methodology, statistics and their limitations is the key. Just as important is the concept of transparency – for any decision made in relation to the preparation or adjustment of data, the reasons for the statistical test used should be clearly presented to the reader.

Critical thinking activity

The file drawer problem: revisited (Rosenthal, 1991)

Critical thinking focus: analysing and evaluating

Key question: *What are the implications of the file drawer problem in relation to our understanding of type I and type II errors?*

As mentioned in Chapter 1, there is an inherent problem in relation to published peer-reviewed research – the file drawer problem. Implicit in most publishable research is that the findings are statistically significant. When statistical non-significance is found, the research, more often than not, finds itself gathering dust in a file drawer (or some part of the hard disk).

Consider the following questions to aid your critical appraisal.

- Upon finding non-significance, what is the use of conducting power analysis?

- What may power analysis tell us?

- If the power was 0.8, is there any use in replicating the study?

Critical thinking review

This activity helps you to develop critical skills in the examination of your own research results. It considers that even though you may have a valid reason for investigation and that your methodology may be faultless (or as much as any methodology can be), you may find non-significance merely as a consequence of the lack of statistical power.

Skill builder activity

Psychological reality versus statistical reality

Transferable skill focus: independent learning

Key question: *To what extent is statistical significance an indicator of psychological usefulness?*

An applied psychologist is interested in testing a new form of memory development training. Two groups are formed: a control group in which no training is given and a test group that undergoes vigorous (and expensive) memory training. Two months later, the psychologist presents a memory task to both groups. It requires the retention of up to 100 facts. Upon completion, there is found to be a statistically significant difference in performance between the two groups in which those who receive the training recall an average of 2.72 more facts than the control group.

Consider the following questions to aid your critical appraisal.

Is the level of significance indicative of the strength of difference between the conditions?

Does the difference in performance warrant the expensive training?

In terms of the difference in recall between the two groups, what difference in the mean number of facts recalled would you consider being of use?

Skill builder review

This activity helps you to build your own independent learning by reflecting on and evaluating the context in which results are demonstrated. Ultimately, it is vital to contextualise your findings in relation to the reality of the situation. Far too often, students become fixated upon the significance of the result and not what that actually (and practically) means.

Assignments

1. The next time you collect data, analyse the first 10, 20, 30 etc. Examine the means and standard deviations as you include more and more data. What do you notice?

2. Consider the following problem. You find non-statistical significance between two conditions but the difference between the means is large. What might be going on?

3. In some areas of psychology, only a few participants are used. How might this lack of data be compensated?

Hint: these participants often spend large amounts of time being tested. Would it be of use to compare response patterns between participants? In addition, consider any insight gleaned from earlier chapters.

Further reading

Clark-Carter, D (2010) *Quantitative Psychological Research: The Complete Students Handbook.* 3rd edition. Hove: Psychology Press.

Chapter 10: Going Beyond Description deals nicely with type I and II errors and how the tail of a test is reflected within a normal distribution.

Dancey, CP and Reidy, J (2007) *Statistics Without Maths for Psychology.* 4th edition. Harlow: Pearson.

Chapter 4: Probability, sampling and distributions deals comprehensively with issues of sampling.

Erdfelder, E, Faul, F and Buchner, A (1996) G POWER: A General Power Analysis Program. *Behaviour Research Methods, Instruments, & Computers*, 28 (1), 1–11.

Faul, F, Erdfelder, E, Lang, A-G and Buchner, A (2007). G*Power 3: A Flexible Statistical Power Analysis Program for the Social, Behavioural, and Biomedical Sciences. *Behaviour Research Methods,* 39(2), 175–191.

Faul, F, Erdfelder, E, Buchner, A and Lang, A-G (2009) Statistical Power Analyses Using G*Power 3.1: Tests for Correlation and Regression Analyses. *Behaviour Research Methods,* 41(4), 1149–1160.

The above are useful articles in relation to the use of G-Power.

Tabachnick, BG and Fidell, LS (2001) *Using Multivariate Statistics.* 4th edition. Boston: Allyn & Bacon.

Chapter 4: Cleaning up your act, screening data prior to analysis is an excellent chapter outlining problems associated with missing data and non-normal distributions, and how they can be resolved.

Useful software

G Power. Both Mac OS X and Windows versions. These are available at www.psycho.uni-duesseldorf.de/aap/projects/gpower/

Chapter 12

Report writing

Learning outcomes

This is the final chapter of this book. Likewise, writing a report is the final step for any research project you have been involved with and so makes for a fitting ending. Writing a report is a way for you to communicate your findings and interpretation to a wider audience. Unfortunately, quite often it is apparent that while students put a lot of hard work into the design, testing and analysis of a project, when it comes to the actual writing up they lose the enthusiasm and energy to complete this last requirement and the resultant quality of the report may be somewhat lacking. But it need not be so! The report is the final product, and indeed the only thing to be seen by the reader (or indeed your tutor), so this chapter will spell out the necessity and requirements for each section in a typical research report.

By the end of this chapter you should:

- *be able to list the different sections contained in a research report;*

- *understand how each section differs and why they are necessary;*

- *appreciate the value of including references and appendices;*

- *consider using this chapter as a guide to writing your own reports.*

Report writing

Any research project is a multi-faceted undertaking. After fixing on a subject area and appraising the literature surrounding that area, initially there is a need to consider the research question at hand, i.e. what is the study trying to investigate? Once this has been formalised, you need to design the study carefully, select your IVs and DVs, and plan to avoid any confounding or extraneous variables that may undermine the validity of your study; ethical issues need to be considered; participants need to be sampled, recruited and allocated to groups or conditions in an appropriate fashion; the actual testing needs to be conducted in suitable locations and in a timely fashion; once the data has been collected, the relevant analysis needs to be performed and the findings interpreted in relation to the initial research question and existing literature. Once all this has been achieved, there is a need to disseminate these findings to a wider audience – this is, after all, the main motivating factor that drives research; to further our understanding of a given topic by investigating factors pertinent to it and communicating this new-found knowledge.

There are various ways in which this can be achieved, but the main two formats are:

- an oral or poster presentation at a research conference;

- writing a report article and having this published in a peer-reviewed journal.

Both formats share a common denominator in that they impart the important details of the research study by adhering to a conventional structure. Should you happen to read a journal article, you may notice that particular sections use different terminology, or certain sections seem to have a greater prominence than others. This is just editorial preference – the underlying structure is essentially the same. You may also notice a slight difference between research reports on quantitative and qualitative projects, but as we shall see later on, these differences are, again, variations on a theme; the quintessential structure remains the same. As students, you are taught to use this structure in your laboratory reports.

Sequence of sections in a typical research report

- Title page.

- Abstract.

- Introduction.

- Method.

- Results.

- Discussion.

- References.

- Appendices.

Title page

The title gives the reader the very first clue as to the content of a research article/lab report. By necessity, then, it should be succinct and uncomplicated. Rather than attempting to use a title that is unclear, vague or even comical, the title should be elegant and stated in terms of independent and dependent variables, if appropriate. We advise students to limit the title to around 10 to 15 words in order to ensure a tight focus.

Abstract

This section should be considered as a précis – a clear summary of the entire report written in a single paragraph of approximately 150 to 200 words. The main purpose of the abstract is to give the reader an overview of the report to determine whether it is relevant to their interests and worth reading further. It therefore needs to include a concise account of each section of the report: brief background to the phenomenon of interest, the rudimentary design details, a synopsis of the method, an outline of the main findings being reported (without any statistical evidence – just in words) and a summary of the main conclusions. For this reason, it should be the last section you attempt to write in a lab report.

Introduction

The Introduction is a chance to convey to the reader why the topic being investigated in this project is worthy of research. Initially, there is a requirement to give an account of the background literature in general, before providing a very clear and balanced appraisal of other research studies that are particularly germane to the specific area being investigated. You need to explain the current state of knowledge and theoretical interpretations, and therefore need to base this on contemporary research papers – by that, we mean you should be aiming to include primary sources of information (i.e. research articles that have been published in peer-reviewed journals), ideally from within the last five years.

Any factual statements you make need to be supported by citations (think of these as evidence) from published sources; failing to do this makes your work appear to be subjective, unsupported and scholastically very weak (see Reference section on pages 179–82 for more details). There is a tendency for students to back up their arguments by quoting sentences verbatim from other published studies, the likely motivation being that by using direct quotes it appears to strongly endorse or support the argument better. While it is true that a quote may clarify the issue if it is particularly eloquent (or used as evidence against the original author if it is horribly incorrect), in reality a glut of quotes may be symptomatic of a student not really understanding the central issues and using the quotes as a ploy to disguise their confusion. Instead, you should paraphrase what others have written and convey this clearly in your own words.

Provide a clear structure. By writing the critical review, you should be making it readily apparent to the reader that there are gaps in our knowledge or incompatible theoretical interpretations within the area of interest. This provides the rationale as to why your study can offer a unique contribution to the area investigated, because you are intending to plug this gap and increase understanding of this subject. The Introduction can then be completed with an explanation of the key research questions your study was designed to answer, and what the specific a priori predictions or hypotheses were. Overall, then, the Introduction should have what is often referred to as a 'funnel' shape. It begins with fairly general, broad issues before funnelling down to include pertinent findings from the literature, eventually narrowing its focus on to this individual project – its rationale, specific predictions and hypotheses.

Task ─┐ As an undergraduate, it was spelled out to me that when writing the critical review I was to include published sources within a five-year timeframe. What reasons do you think are given for having such a contemporary selection of journal articles?

Method

This section tells the reader exactly what you did in this investigation. It is of paramount importance that you convey sufficiently detailed information so that someone reading your report could go ahead and replicate your study (and hopefully duplicate your findings, thus strengthening the validity and reliability of your original investigation). Unfortunately, there is a tendency among some to underestimate the importance of the Method section and provide scant details. After all, you know what you did, but quite often this is not conveyed adequately.

Four subsections are typically used.

- Participants.

- Design.

- Materials.

- Procedure.

Participants

Unless you have conducted a case study of an individual person, you will have recruited a number of people to participate in your research study. It is therefore important that you provide relevant information regarding your participants. How many were there? What were their demographic details (for example, age, gender)? Were any participants deliberately excluded? Did any drop out? Why did they withdraw? How did you sample your participants? These details need to be conveyed so others may ascertain the reliability and validity of your investigation.

Design

This section requires that you stipulate the formal design features of your study. So if you used an experimental investigation, you would need to state the precise design that was implemented. Was it between-participants or cross-sectional (i.e. different groups of participants), repeated-measures or longitudinal (one group of participants tested numerous times), a combination of the two (mixed factorial or sequential), or was it a correlational/regression design (looking at the association or predictive relationship between two or more variables)? Refer to Chapters 4, 5 and 6 to refresh your understanding of these designs. You should also include reference to the independent variables manipulated in this study, and what dependent variables were used to measure this experimentation. Depending on the design considerations, you could state how you counter-balanced or randomised the conditions (see Chapter 4). This presents the design information in a clear-cut and concise manner that facilitates comprehension of what exactly was undertaken and eases any desire to replicate the study.

Task — Suppose you conducted a study that employed a mixed 3*(2) factorial design. From this information, you should be able to ascertain the number of between- and within-participant variables, the number of levels in both of these and the total number of conditions in this study. See if you can do this.

Materials

What materials, stimuli or apparatus were included in this investigation? Do not fall into the trap of simply listing these instruments as though they were ingredients in a culinary dish. Nor should you state how they were used – that comes in the Procedure section (next). You need to provide specific details about these resources: if you used questionnaires, state who the authors are and when they were published; stipulate how many items (questions) it contains; give examples of these items and the response scales (Likert, semantic differentials, ratings); give information as to published indices of validity and reliability. If you used a computer to display visual or auditory images, how were these stimuli selected? State the software and version used to display these. What was the size and resolution of the screen? What was the volume and distance sat from the screen? Provide the pertinent relevant details to the area under investigation; room temperature and humidity may not be relevant to studies measuring reaction times to emotionally provoking stimuli, but they are if you were recording skin conductivity.

Procedure

This section is probably the most straightforward. You can explain how your participants were assigned to different experimental conditions; give a summary of the verbal and/or written instructions given to all your participants; describe the order of events presented in the study and any indications how long this lasted. You should also communicate how your participants were debriefed after completing the study. Describing with clarity and transparency the events of your investigation, with sufficient detail, is absolutely vital for the reader to understand what happened.

Some students (and journal authors) may forget the magnitude of this subsection and confuse the reader, thus ultimately undermining the impact of their own investigation.

Results (Analysis and Discussion in qualitative reports)

Briefly, this section is where you present the findings from your analysis of the data. You are not supposed to interpret your results (that is, for the Discussion), but merely describe and present the results. Depending on the extent of the investigation, the Results can be shortest but also the most infuriatingly difficult section to write.

Initially, you should specify exactly what data was collected. How was this raw data handled? Did it require any preparation for analysis, such as reversal of the scoring scale on particular items from a questionnaire? Did data have to be transformed in order to demonstrate a normal distribution? Were there any statistical outliers in the data? How were missing data points rectified (see Chapter 11 on common problems)? Did the raw data require some other treatment or calculation process in order to provide the scores for subsequent analysis? Do not include the raw data itself – you should not expect that your reader will wade through reams of figures in order to get a grasp of your results.

In order to describe your data and so facilitate an understanding of patterns or trends emerging from your quantitative data, it is expected that you provide a useful summary of scores. This can be achieved via the use of descriptive statistics, such as the mean average and standard deviation for your different groups and/or conditions. You may decide to use tables or graphs (aka 'Figures') to explicitly communicate your results. Make sure that these tables and figures have the group conditions labelled appropriately – the lack of labels (or using terms such as 'Group A') will only serve to muddle your results and potentially confuse the reader. One error we see occasionally is duplication of results: the results section may contain a table of descriptive statistics, a graph will depict the exact same information in visual form, and again the same descriptive statistics will be repeated in text in the main body of results.

Task — Duplication of results is often seen when students have few scores to present, and thus depict the same findings in different forms in order to pad out what they may consider to be a rather anaemic Results section. Why is this perspective untrue?

The next part (for quantitative data) is to report the inferential statistical analysis. What test was employed and on which variables? Were the assumptions for this inferential technique actually met (for example, for between-participant designs was there homogeneity of variance? In regression analyses was there evidence of multicolinearity?) You need to describe what the inferential analysis has indicated – simply cutting and pasting a table outputted from your analysis software is wholly insufficient, as is merely reporting the p-values. You need to describe in words what the analysis actually means in relation to your investigation. The statistical evidence for this (the outcome from the inferential analysis), needs to be presented in the conventional format as taught in statistics modules. Rather than detail all of this here, we refer you to a suitable statistics book for guidance on presenting this statistical evidence.

In short, report everything relevant to your research question or hypotheses and provide enough detail for the reader to draw their own conclusions. After all, your conclusion may not necessarily be the correct one . . . though hopefully it is!

Discussion (Summary and Conclusion in qualitative reports)

The Discussion section is where you make sense of your findings. Initially, you should simply restate the main findings from your investigation, devoid of any statistical evidence as you need to be clear and succinct about what you have uncovered. A good Discussion should make sense, even when it has been isolated from the rest of the report (if anyone is interested in the analysis on which you have based your interpretation, or the methods used, then they can read the appropriate sections).

After the initial presentation of the findings, it is important that they are interpreted in relation to the predictions/hypotheses set out in the Introduction. This can then be further elaborated on in reference to the existing literature (including studies not cited in your Introduction). How exactly do your findings fit in with earlier studies and theories? Are they congruent? Might they offer a contrasting pattern of results? Regardless of which it is, what then might be the implications of this consistent/conflicting support? Overall, what are the ramifications for the state of knowledge and understanding of the research topic under investigation? Might there be a need for a reassessment of existing theories and constructs? Perhaps existing theories can be consolidated, or need to be modified in light of current findings – or can even be rejected if your results warrant it? Ideas for future directions of research should also be made. What new studies can be considered, or which additional variables should be taken into account next time? Might clinical groups or different aged-cohorts be worth investigating?

It is incumbent upon you to evaluate the relative merits and contribution of your own study. In the critical review of the literature provided in the Introduction, you assess the evidence gleaned from many different published sources relating to the topic under investigation. It is only right and proper, therefore, that you appraise your own study. In this subsection, we might expect to see a discussion of limitations stemming from the current investigation – for example, an evaluation of the design and procedure, or an acknowledgement of issues that arose during the testing or analysis stage that may have implications for the subsequent interpretation of findings (see Chapter 11 for discussion of common problems). Transparency should be evident – as stated in

Chapters 1 and 11, there is no such thing as a perfect study. Not all variables can be controlled and accounted for, and it is inevitable that certain problems may surface in a study – the skill is in minimising the extent and effect of these.

The final paragraph in this section should contain an abridged version of the main conclusions in order to provide an overall summary of the research investigation that has just been presented. This is often omitted from student lab reports, either due to forgetting or the constraint of the page limit imposed on the assignment. Do not forget to do this – it is an opportunity to provide a bite-sized synopsis of your project and leave a favourable impression upon the reader.

Task — Providing a critique of your own investigation is to be expected in a research report (indeed, it is a sign of a poor journal if you read a published article that does not contain this). However, in lab reports based on experiments that fail to reject the null hypothesis (i.e. have no 'significant' results), we often find that students seem to systematically deconstruct and annihilate their own study with severe criticisms at all levels. Why do you think this is, and is a non-significant result any less informative than a significant result?

References

In various sections throughout the report (but mainly in the Introduction and Discussion), you should have made reference to existing studies that provide evidential support for or against a particular supposition. These are known as citations. In the References section, you are expected to present a formatted list of all citations used in your report. This enables someone reading your report to locate and access a particular study you cited in order to weigh up the evidence for themselves.

Whenever you are reproducing someone else's words, or citing someone else's ideas or research findings, you must always make it clear to whom the words, ideas or findings belong. Failure to credit the original author(s) cannot be simply written off as borrowing or copying – instead, it can be construed as plagiarism, the deliberate fraudulent act of using someone else's work and passing it off as your own original effort. This is perhaps the most serious accusation that can be levied against an academic and the penalties can effectively end your career as a researcher. Many universities now employ computer software programs that have algorithms sensitive enough to identify similarities between submitted assignments and existing resources both online (such as electronic journal articles, websites) and offline (such as book chapters and previously submitted student assignments). You have been warned!

There are many different methods of referencing used in journals and books, but the three main types most commonly used in psychological journals are the American Psychiatric Association

(APA), Harvard and Chicago systems. They are, to all intents and purposes, identical (bar very minor differences) and all three use what is termed an author–date format. Whenever a citation is given, details of the pertinent study are given there and then in parentheses (brackets) in the text rather than appearing as footnotes or endnotes. The citation itself simply consists of the author(s) and year of publication. Should a direct quote be used, then the citation must include the page number(s) the quote can be found on in the original paper.

As an example:

Richardson et al. (2009, p18) indicated that *"trauma memory during nontherapeutic mental replay is mainly in working memory in dorsolateral areas of the prefrontal cortex, consistent with the clinical experience that simple rehearsal of the details of the trauma is not rapidly helpful"*.

In the Reference section, this cited journal article would appear as:

Richardson, P, Williams, SR, Hepenstall, S, Gregory, L, McKie, S and Corrigan, F (2009) A Single-Case fMRI Study: EMDR Treatment of a Patient with Posttraumatic Stress Disorder. *Journal of EMDR Practice and Research*, 3(1), 10–23.

Surname, Initial(s) (Year) Title of paper, Name of Journal in Italics with Main Words in Capitals. Volume number (Issue number), inclusive pages.

A book would appear as:

Baddeley, AD (1990) *Human Memory: Theory and Practice*. Erlbaum Associates, Hove, UK.

Surname, Initial(s) (Year) Title in italics. Publisher, Place of publication.

Books and journal articles should be amalgamated and listed alphabetically in a joint References section; you should not have a separate list depending on the type of source used. This includes the use of websites – a recent and growing trend found in student assignments. Nor should you include a Bibliography – this is a list of sources that have been read and have informed your writing. This does not accurately reflect the stated purpose and intent of a list of cited references and is to be avoided. Similarly, you should not include publications in your reference list that you have failed to cite in the report (or essay even), nor should you cite publications in your report without including them in your reference list. This is indicative of a substandard and unscholarly level of work.

As you may surmise, one obvious advantage of reference systems using the author–date format is that you can quickly become familiar with, and recognise, individual citations (so much so that you may even find yourself not having to sift through the references in order to locate the study in question). Key papers can then be readily acknowledged by the reader and, for contrasting reasons, poorly executed studies (or those that have since been retracted) can also be spotted quickly. In addition, being able to spot the year of publication within the text permits the reader (and marking tutor) to easily identify citations that are not contemporary and especially outdated. Reference systems that use a numerical format (such as Wikipedia and in the example below) do not permit such impressions of the work.

An example would be:

> *The parietal area has reciprocal connections with the posterior cingulate cortex and may be important for visual imagery associated with memory recall (1). The left parahippocampal gyrus has been implicated in another study of episodic autobiographical memory (2).*

In this system, the full reference is given later in the same ascending numerical order as it appears in the text. Unfortunately, this means that the reader has to flip back and forth to the references in order to determine who wrote what. While this may slow you down should you wish to identify the credited sources, you may find that reading the text is somewhat easier as it is not punctuated by multiple author and date citations interrupting your flow.

Appendices

The Appendices of your lab report contain materials you may have discussed in your Materials section. You may include examples of questionnaires, visual stimuli, tests used, written instructions and any information/debrief sheets handed to your participants. You may also include statistical output so that your tutor can ensure it is correct. In journal articles, the Appendices may also include supplementary information not directly pertinent to the paper and so not included in the text; these may include additional analyses or demographic material. Any materials in the Appendices need to be individually labelled and specifically referred to in your report.

Critical thinking activity

Transparency and honesty in research

Critical thinking focus: reflection

Key question: *Can we trust researchers?*

It is not necessary to include your raw data or statistical output in the Appendices of your research report when submitting for publication (though tutors may expect to see the latter simply to confirm you have interpreted it correctly). The reason for this is that it is taken on trust that you have been honest and above board, and that the data (and subsequent analysis) is correct. However, you are obliged to share this analysis when requested to do so. Research and Development Boards (these cover projects involving, among others, NHS patients), in accordance with stricter research governance initiatives stipulated by the Department of Health, are obliged to monitor a minimum of ten per cent of all research projects per year. Do you consider this policy to be sufficient?

Critical thinking review

This question rears up every now and again. Can we trust researchers, or indeed any profession, to independently police themselves? Should we encourage an environment of micromanagement in which the minutiae of every single research study is examined thoroughly in order to root out the falsified data, spurious findings and results regurgitated in different journals? Might this create a set of unwieldy financial and administrative burdens? As imperfect as the current system is, it may be the one most appropriate to research.

Having you sit and reflect on these issues is of paramount importance. Too often students simply accept at face value what they are told in lectures or read in books. Get out of that passive habit! You need to cogitate and think through the implications and consequences of any information with which you are being presented. Challenge yourself.

Skill builder activity

Peer review

Transferable skill focus: teamwork

Key question: *Does peer review actually work?*

One process currently in vogue in many university departments is to require students to undertake a peer review once they have written their assignments (but not yet submitted these for formal marking). This is simply where we have students swap lab reports with each other during a session and provide a critical review of each section. What possible advantages could stem from such an activity? Quite often it is suggested to students that they ask friends studying on courses outside of psychology to read through their assignments. Why might this be?

Skill builder review

The rationale behind peer reviews is twofold. First, psychology students are presented with an opportunity to hone their critiquing skills. This is a key attribute that is a prerequisite not only for any career in psychology, but also beneficial in everyday occupational and social settings. Depending on the importance of the situation, it should be tacitly acknowledged that you do not accept information you are told on an unconditional basis. You should require evidence that supports this information, and this exercise is a great way to exercise your ability to appraise information.

The flip side of this activity is that students simultaneously may also provide, and thus in return will receive, valuable suggestions as to how they may improve their assignment ready for submission. By acting on these suggestions (or by virtue of spotting something in another student's document), the idea is that they will improve their own work accordingly. Furthermore, the suggestion of having a non-psychology student (or family member) proofread the work is valuable because their lack of knowledge of the topic means they are more likely to spot sections of text that are incoherent, rambling and simply do not make sense. This is especially true of the Method section – you may well be fully conversant with all facets of the project you spent umpteen hours working on, but quite often this is not conveyed in a clear and straightforward manner.

Assignments

1. When critically reviewing the literature in the Introduction, many students are tempted to praise the studies that promote theoretical positions that are supportive of the findings from their own investigation, while studies that suggest alternative interpretations or have produced incompatible findings are somewhat unfairly critiqued and denigrated. Why should this 'patch-protection' be avoided at all costs?

2. The critical review of the literature should be evaluative, not merely a superficial description of each study and its findings. The relative contribution each study makes to the understanding of the subject area needs to be assessed. How, then, might you critique published studies? What details should you include?

3. Primary sources of information include published journal articles written by the author(s) that report findings of an individual investigation (or possibly a small collection of linked studies). It may also include specialist texts or monographs, but will not include secondary sources of information such as introductory textbooks in which the authors write about a variety of topics

under a common theme (for example, developmental psychology) and include findings from a variety of research studies conducted by others. Why not?

Summary: what you have learned

In this chapter, you were reminded of why we undertake research – so that we may enhance our understanding of how key variables influence the topic we are investigating. By reporting back the findings of these research studies, we can communicate this knowledge to others in the same field so that collectively more is learned about the subject matter at hand. This chapter concentrated on the most common method of disseminating the findings from such investigations – writing a research report.

We presented the basic layout of a research report, and stipulated the reasoning behind why each section needs completing and what you should consider including in each of these sections and subsections.

Do not think of this chapter as a blueprint or template, or the suggested word limits as sacrosanct scripture – instead, view it as an informative guide to assist you in the writing up of a lab report, an experience that need not be one to dread.

Further reading

Field, A and Hole, G (2003) *How to Design and Report Experiments*. London: Sage.

This book has extremely well written and detailed chapters on reporting and writing up research investigations.

University of Washington (2010) *APA Style Citations & References: A Guide for Psychology Undergraduates*. Available for free download from http://web.psych.washington.edu/writingcenter/writingguides/pdf/citations.pdf [Last accessed 11 May 2011]

This pdf file is a more detailed guide on the APA reference/citation system and is well worth a read due to the myriad of different citation methods that exist. It also contains a useful exercise on formatting references.

Glossary

alternative
hypothesis

see *experimental hypothesis*.

alternate/parallel

referring to a version of a test that is similar to the original. This ensures the same construct is being assessed to a similar level, but it is sufficiently different so as to avoid instances of practice effects (i.e. performance on subsequent testing will increase merely due to repeating the original test).

approximate value

this is a term that refers to the measuring accuracy of any instrument/task. While it may be possible to measure reaction time to 1,000,000th of a second – in reality, this degree of accuracy is not required or indeed useful. A less precise figure will suffice.

attrition

the loss of participants from a study – either due to their purposeful with-drawal or loss of contact. This loss can be random (in which each condition experiences a loss of similar numbers of participants) or non-random – in which a particular condition(s) may be affected more than others.

between-
participants

an experimental design that utilises different groups of different people. Each group experiences a different condition but is tested on the same measure, thus any effects can be compared easily.

bias

an unwanted effect in which performance of participants may be affected somehow.

carry-over effect

performance on later trials or conditions may be affected by experiences gleaned from earlier trials. This is why the order of conditions should be randomly sorted for participants.

case study

an investigation in which the sample size is of a single individual. Having n=1 enables a more intensive and detailed examination of any relevant aspect of the participant's behaviour.

category

a term used to classify a grouping of levels within some variable.

causal inference

a cause-and-effect link between the manipulation of an IV and the resultant changes as demonstrated on the DV.

central limit
theorem

a theorem based on probability theory – it is the propensity of data (given sufficient sample size and variance) to be normally distributed.

cohort

a group of similarly aged participants.

complementarity	a feature of mixed methods research in which data derived from one method is used in conjunction with data derived from an alternative method in order to complement and enhance the interpretability and significance of results obtained.
concurrent validity	a correlated measure of how consistent one instrument is with another instrument that purports to measure the same construct (for example, two depression questionnaires).
confounding variable	an unwanted variable that changes simultaneously with the manipulated changes in the IV. The net result is that you cannot state which variable caused the observed effect.
construct	a psychological entity that cannot be measured directly, such as 'courage' or 'extroversion'.
constructivist	refers to a philosophical position that holds that we each 'construct' our own unique understanding of our world, based on our experiences and on rules we develop in order to make sense of these.
continuous variable	a variable whose levels can (theoretically) be infinitely small – for example, reactions times can be measured in units that themselves are composed of smaller units ad infinitum.
control condition	a condition in an experiment in which the participants receive no level of the IV. For instance, they receive 0mg/kg of caffeine in contrast to those in the experimental condition, who receive 20mg/kg.
correlation coefficient	a scale varying from ±1 to 0 that indicates both the direction and strength of an association between two variables.
counterbalance, complete and partial	in research studies using repeated-measures variable(s), the order in which conditions are presented to each participant need to be varied so as to avoid order effects. There are complete and partial forms of counterbalancing, the first of which requires all conditions to be randomised for all participants; the latter is less strict.
co-variance	the degree to which changes in levels of one variable coincide with changes in levels of another variable – for example, the amount of chocolate I eat and the size of my waist.
Cronbach's alpha	a measure of internal reliability often used in questionnaire design. It provides an index as to the extent to which all the items are measuring the same construct.

cross-sectional design	a research design in which cohorts (groups of similarly aged participants) are compared with each other to specifically test age-related differences.
cross-sequential design	a research design that combines both cross-sectional and longitudinal methods.
deductive reasoning	a line of reasoning that argues that a conclusion is valid if it follows logically from an original hypothesis that can be tested. Contrast with *inductive*.
degree of association	the extent to which changes in two variables coincide.
demand characteristics	a situation in which participants (unwittingly or not) may alter their natural behaviour or performance levels to be consistent with what they think is expected of them.
dependent variable (DV)	a variable that is used to measure the effect of manipulating another variable – for example, using a heart rate monitor to assess the dosage levels of a beta-blocker drug.
discrete variable	a variable that has definitive 'stop-start' levels that are not composed of ever smaller subunits.
discursive devices	discursive devices are features that occur in language. Devices achieve, or help to achieve, some level of action. They should not be thought of as conscious strategies, but as elements that are embedded in our language culture.
double-blind study	a study that ensures that both participants and researchers are unaware as to what group or condition they are in. This is to ensure there is no potential to leak information or bias the results.
ecological validity	a position that any tasks or testing conditions should be as close to 'real life' as possible, otherwise the results are arguably an artificial contrivance.
exclusive	refers to variables that use categories. Each category must be distinct from each other and only one category can be chosen as a response – for example, what is your favourite primary colour: blue, red OR yellow?
exhaustive	refers to a property of categorical variables, which posits that all possible responses/categories need to be used – for example, if we asked people to tick their political preferences on a questionnaire, we would need to list all the political parties.
expansion	a feature of research studies employing mixed methods. By using a mixture of different approaches, the range of enquiry is expanded and additional results can be obtained.

expectancy effects	a situation in which a participant's expectation of what they might experience will affect their true reaction to it.
experimental conditions	in an experimental research design, the independent variable is manipulated to different levels, thus creating a series of different conditions to be tested. For example, the effects of 0, 10, 20 and 30 ml/kg of alcohol on driving performance: this study has three experimental conditions and one control condition (0ml/kg).
experimental hypothesis	a statement in which the different levels of an independent variable will cause a change in the dependent variable.
experimenter expectancy	in which the experimenter unconsciously influences the results of the experiment.
external validity	the extent to which the findings can be related to the population under examination.
extraneous variable	any variable that may potentially affect the outcome of an experiment to a small degree and makes a nuisance of itself, but does not jeopardise the research (see Chapter 4 for more details).
face validity	a subjective evaluation of how the participant perceives a particular measurement.
field notes	field notes are a comprehensive and clear set of notes that describe the action or situation being observed in observation studies. They should be detailed enough that they carry sufficient information for someone who was not present at the observation to have clear understanding of it.
Gaussian distribution	in probability theory this relates to normal distribution.
heterogeneity of variance	this is where the spread of data around a mean across the different experimental conditions is similar enough to be considered as the same for all conditions.
homogeneity of variance	this is where the spread of data around a mean across the different experimental conditions is similar enough to be considered as the same for all conditions.
incompatibility thesis	the argument that qualitative and quantitative research methods are irreconcilably different and should not be mixed in a single study.
independent variable (IV)	a variable whose levels are purposefully manipulated in order to test the effects these different levels may have on some measure (the DV).

inductive	refers to a form of reasoning in which theories are formed based on observation of a singular or individual event. Contrast with *deductive reasoning*.
infer	to draw a conclusion based on evidence.
initiation	a process in which the seemingly contradictory results of one method are used as a basis to question and reformulate the approach of another method.
inter-coder reliability	a measure of reliability often used in qualitative studies, particularly in observation studies. The use of multiple coders or observers is very useful. By using several coders, the risk of overly subjective interpretation can be reduced. By ensuring that features are viewed by more than one coder, they can be seen as valid.
inter-item	refers to a measure of reliability often used in questionnaire design. It assesses the extent to which all items correlate with each other, and thus measure the same construct.
internal validity	the extent to which causality can be inferred. See Chapter 1.
inter-rater	refers to the extent to which two raters are concordant in their rating of any given variable of interest – for example, using the same questionnaire, is their rating of an individual's behaviour in agreement? Also see *inter-coder reliability*.
interval	according to Stevens (1946), there are four levels of measurement. A variable with an interval level has scales that are equidistant but has no absolute zero – think of a thermometer!
interview schedule	the interview schedule is the most important tool in the running of interviews. It should be carefully constructed and piloted before being used on a larger sample.
laboratory settings	a research setting using rooms or booths that are free from distracting stimuli. This tight control of events mimics laboratories associated with the physical science.
Latin-squares design	a process in which the presentation order of conditions in an experiment are systematically varied so as to avoid the confounding order effects.
levels of measurement	a position advocated by Stevens (1946) that argues that variables have four levels of measurement, each increasing in complexity of features. See also *nominal*, *ordinal*, *interval level* and *ratio*.
longitudinal design	a research design used in developmental psychology to assess the effect of age on some variable. One cohort of participants are tested repeatedly over

an extended time frame – for example, at age 7, 10, 13 and 16 years. This is akin to a within-participants design.

magnitude	size or extent.
manipulation	refers to the systematic alternation of the independent variable (IV) in experimental research to produce different levels. This manipulation is designed to permit the examination of the effect these different levels have on the dependent variable (DV).
matched pairs	refers to a design in which you attempt to pair up a participant from one group with a participant from the other, having matched them as closely as possible on a selection of variables such as age, IQ, handedness or gender.
microgenetic design	an intensive longitudinal study over a very short duration designed to assess a particular skill as it is developing.
mixed factorial design	a design that permits two or more variables to be simultaneously investigated using a combination of between- and within-participant designs. (Simple experiments involve the testing of one independent variable (factor) that necessitates using either a between-participants or within-participants design.)
mixed methods	the use of multiple methods in research, most often associated with using quantitative and qualitative approaches.
moderator and *mediator variables*	variables that influence the degree of association between two other variables (moderator), and that actually account for the relationship between two other variables (mediator).
natural (or field) environments	a research setting that is not the laboratory, but a real-world setting.
negative relationship	a type of association between two variables: as the value of one increases, the other decreases – for example, drinking alcohol and accuracy of driving.
nocebo effect	a set of unpleasant side effects from ingesting a placebo treatment. The belief that this treatment/pill may cause negative side effects may be enough to precipitate them – despite the pill itself being inert.
nominal	describes the simplest level of measurement. Such variables are made up of discrete categories that in themselves have no intrinsic value – for example, colours.
null hypothesis	simply a statement that there is no effect of the levels of an independent variable upon the dependent variable.

operational definition	an explicit statement of the parameters used in answering the research question.
operationalise	to clearly define.
opportunistic sampling	a sampling method where participants are recruited through the most convenient method possible.
ordinal	the second level of measurement. Such variables are made up of discrete categories, but they can be ranked according to some order – for example, 1st, 2nd or 3rd in a race.
outlier	a data point that is extreme in relation to the data set collected.
paradigm wars	a major dispute between the proponents of qualitative and quantitative research methods.
parametric modulation	a reference to a systematic and graduated manipulation of the levels of an independent variable – for example, levels of alcohol in an experiment could be set at 0%, 5%, 10%, 15% and 20% concentrations, rather than the ad hoc basis of 0%, 5% and 20%.
parametric test	an inferential test in which certain parameters are specified as being essential or desirable for their use.
placebo	a dummy pill (or solution) given to participants that is metabolically inert but indistinguishable from the real pill being studied, and so helps guard against experimenter bias and demand characteristics. It is usually made from simple sugars.
population	a group defined by the research question that indicates the parameters of those from which you are going to sample.
positive relationship	a type of association between two variables: as the value of one increases, so too does the value of the other – for example, drinking alcohol and number of driving mistakes.
positivist	a philosophical belief that only knowledge gained through the scientific method can be authentic.
power	the likelihood of avoiding a type II error.
pragmatist approach	the firm belief that research questions cannot be answered solely by quantitative or qualitative methods, and therefore a 'whatever works' mixed methods is the best approach.

pre- and post-test design	refers to an experimental design in which it is possible to measure the effects of some intervention on a test by comparing participants' scores on the test taken before and after the intervention.
predictive validity	the extent to which the measure predicts the outcome.
quantifying	assigning a numerical value to some construct, so that it then varies.
quota convenience sampling	a sampling method where a desired number of participants are recruited through the most convenient method possible.
random allocation	this is where participants have an equal chance to be allocated to any of the experimental conditions.
random error	a bias in measurement that is not consistent; the degree of bias varies and may, in fact, at times not be present.
random sampling	this is where all those within a specific population have an equal chance of being selected as a participant.
rank-ordered	the sorting of scores or levels of a variable according to ascending value, i.e. 1st lowest, 2nd lowest, 3rd lowest etc.
ratio	the fourth and final level of measurement. Such variables have scales that are anchored by a true zero (for example, 0cm), thus permitting ratio comparisons, for example, 220msec is twice as long as 110msec.
regression	data analysis technique in which it is possible to see if variables can be used to predict the value of another variable.
reliability	the degree to which the measure does not change over time or successive measurements.
repeated-measures	an experimental design in which the same assessments are given repeatedly in different conditions. See *within-participants*.
research question	in qualitative methods there is no use of a hypothesis, as the methods are generally inductive in nature. Instead of using a hypothesis, the research formulates a research question around the topic in which they are interested.
scatterplots	a simple graph that plots participant's scores on two variables on two axes, thus visually depicting the direction (and rough indicator) as to the strength of this relationship.
single-subject	see *case study*.

Solomon four-group design	a complex experimental design in which it is possible to compare groups of participants who have not experienced any pre-intervention testing.
split-half reliability	a method of assessing the internal reliability of a test by splitting it into two halves and correlating them – for example, odd- versus even-numbered items on a questionnaire.
systematic error	a bias in measurement which is consistent with each measurement.
test-retest reliability	a method of gauging the extent of reliability by comparing scores on the same test taken at two separate time points and correlating them.
time-lagged design	a design format in which it is possible to test people from different generations when they reach the same age. See Chapter 5.
triangulation	a proposed benefit of mixed methodology – by using multiple approaches it entails that a more accurate and informative research programme is conducted.
type I error	this is the rejection of the null hypothesis when, in fact, it is true. In other words, deciding that there is an effect of levels of an independent variable upon the dependent variable. Normally, the likelihood of making a type I error is five per cent (p=.05)
type II error	this is the likelihood of failing to reject the null hypothesis when, in fact, one should. In other words, it is failing to determine that there is a difference between the levels of an independent variable upon the dependent variable. The probability of making this error is dependent upon the power level.
validity	the extent to which you can be sure that you are measuring what is intended.
variable	some property of an event, or person, that will have different values at different times depending on the conditions – for example, colours, height, attitude, extroversion.
within-participants	an experimental design that uses one group of participants and exposes them to all the conditions within the experiment. See *repeated-measures*.

References

Antaki, C and Widdicombe, S (eds) (1998) *Identities In Talk*. London: Sage.

Baltes, PB (1968) Longitudinal and Cross-Sectional Sequences in the Study of Age and Generation Effects. *Human Development*, 11(3), 145–171.

Bazeley, P (1999) The *Bricoleur* With a Computer: Piecing Together Qualitative and Quantitative Data. *Qualitative Health Research,* 9(2), 279–287.

Benneworth, K (2009) Police Interviews With Suspected Paedophiles: A Discourse Analysis. *Discourse and Society*, 20(5), 555–569.

Billig, M (1991) *Ideology And Opinions: Studies In Rhetorical Psychology*. London: Sage.

Braun, V and Clarke, V (2006) Using Thematic Analysis in Psychology. *Qualitative Research in Psychology*, 3(2), 77–101.

British Psychological Society (2009) *BPS Code of Ethics and Conduct*. Available online at www.bps.org.uk/the-society/code-of-conduct/code-of-conduct_home.cfm [Accessed 2 April 2011]

Buchanan, D and Bryman, A (2007) Contextualizing Methods Choice in Organizational Research. *Organizational Research Methods*, 10(3), 483–501.

Cameron, R and Miller, P (2007) Mixed Method Research: Phoenix of the Paradigm Wars. *Proceedings of 21st Annual Australian and New Zealand Academy of Management (ANZAM) Conference*, Sydney, 4–7 December.

Campbell, DT and Fiske, DW (1959) Convergent and Discriminant Validation by the Multitrait-multimethod Matrix. *Psychological Bulletin,* 56(2), 81–105.

Charmaz, K (2008) Grounded Theory, in Smith, JA (ed) *Qualitative Psychology: A Practical Guide to Research Methods.* 2nd edition. London: Sage.

Clark-Carter, D (2010) *Quantitative Psychological Research: The Complete Student's Handbook*. Hove: Psychology Press.

Cohen, J (1988) *Statistical Power Analysis for the Behavioural Sciences.* 2nd edition. Hillsdale, NJ: Lawrence Erlbaum Associates.

Cook, TD and Campbell, DT (1979) *Quasi-Experimentation: Design and Analysis for Field Settings*. Chicago, Illinois: Rand McNally.

Dancey, CP and Reidy, J (2007) *Statistics Without Maths for Psychology*. 4th edition. Harlow: Pearson Education.

Dancey, C and Reidy, J (2011) *Statistics Without Maths for Psychology*. 5th edition. Harlow: Prentice Hall.

Danner, F and Phillips, B (2008) Adolescent Sleep, School Start Times and Teen Motor Vehicle Crashes. *Journal of Clinical Sleep Medicine*, 4(6), 533–535.

Denzin, NK (ed) (1978) *Sociological Methods: A Sourcebook*. New York: McGraw-Hill.

Edwards, D (1997) *Discourse and Cognition*. London: Sage.

Edwards, D and Potter, J (1992) *Discursive Psychology*. London: Sage.

Gershkoff-Stowe, L and Smith, LB (1997) A Curvilinear Trend in Naming Errors as a Function of Early Vocabulary Growth. *Cognitive Psychology*, 34, 37–71.

Giddings, LS (2006) Mixed-methods Research: Positivism Dressed in Drag? *Journal of Research in Nursing*, 11(3), 195–203.

Glaser, BG and Strauss, AL (1967) *The Discovery of Grounded Theory: Strategies for Qualitative Research*. Chicago: Aldine Publishing Company.

Gould, SJ (1981) *The Mismeasure of Man*. 2nd edition. New York: WW Norton and Company.

Greene, JC and Caracelli, VJ (eds) (1997) *Advances in Mixed-method Evaluation: The Challenges and Benefits of Integrating Diverse Paradigms* (New Directions for Evaluation, No. 74). San Francisco: Jossey-Bass.

Greene, JC, Caracelli, VJ and Graham, WF (1989) Toward a Conceptual Framework for Mixed-Method Evaluation Designs. *Educational Evaluation and Policy Analysis*, 11(3), 255–274.

Guttman, L (1944) A Basis for Scaling Quantitative Data. *American Sociological Review*, 9(2), 139–150.

Happé, F and Frith, U (1996) Theory of Mind and Social Impairment in Children with Conduct Disorder. *British Journal of Developmental Psychology*, 14(4), 385–398.

Howe, KR (1988) Against the Quantitative–Qualitative Incompatibility Thesis or Dogmas Die Hard. *Educational Researcher,* 17(8), 10–16.

Humphrey, L (1970) *Tearoom Trade: A Study of Homosexual Encounters in Public Places*. London: Duckworth.

Jefferson, G (2004) Glossary of Transcription Symbols with an Introduction, in Learner, G (ed) *Conversation Analysis: Studies From The First Generation*. Philadelphia: John Benjamins.

Johnson, RB and Onwuegbuzie, AJ (2004) Mixed Methods Research: A Research Paradigm Whose Time Has Come. *Educational Researcher*, 33(7), 14–26.

Johnson, RB, Onwuegbuzie, AJ and Turner, LA (2007) Toward a Definition of Mixed Methods Research. *Journal of Mixed Methods Research*, 1(2), 112–133.

Jones, H (1981) *Bad Blood: The Tuskegee Syphilis Experiment*. New York: Free Press.

Judd, CM, Smith, ER and Kidder, LH (1991) *Research Methods in Social Relations*. London: Harcourt College Publishers.

Kline, P (2000) *The Handbook of Psychological Testing*. 2nd edition. London: Routledge.

Likert, R (1932) A Technique for the Measurement of Attitudes. *Archives of Psychology,* 140(20), 1–55.

Luce, RD and Tukey, JW (1964) Simultaneous Conjoint Measurement: A New Scale Type of Fundamental Measurement. *Journal of Mathematical Psychology*, 1(1), 1–27.

Luce, RD, Krantz, DH, Suppes, P and Tversky, A (1990) *Foundations of Measurement, Vol. III: Representation, Axiomatization, and Invariance*. New York: Academic Press.

Matthews, R (2000) Storks Deliver Babies (p=0.008). *Teaching Statistics*, 22(2), 36–38.

Mertins, D and Ginsberg, P (2009) *The Handbook of Social Research Ethics*. London: Sage.

Michell, J (1997) Quantitative Science and the Definition of Measurement in Psychology. *British Journal of Psychology*, 88, 355–383.

Milgram, S (1963) Behavioral Study of Obedience. *Journal of Abnormal and Social Psychology*, 67(4), 371–78.

Milgram, S (1974) *Obedience to Authority: An Experimental View*. London: HarperCollins.

Moon, J and Moon, S (2004) The Case for Mixed Methodology Research: A Review of Literature and Methods. A Working Paper. Available online at www.e-mel.co.uk/Mixed%20methodology.pdf

Morse, JM (1991) Approaches to Qualitative–Quantitative Methodological Triangulation. *Nursing Research,* 40(2), 120–123.

Osgood, CE, Suci, CJ and Tannenbaum, PH (1957) *The Measurement of Meaning*. Urbana: University of Illinois Press.

Pallant, J (2010) *SPSS Survival Manual*. 4th edition. Maidenhead: Open University Press.

Potter, J (1996) *Representing Reality*. London: Sage.

Potter, J and Wetherell, M (1987) *Discourse and Social Psychology: Beyond Attitudes and Behaviour*. London: Sage.

Rosenberg, MJ (1965) When Dissonance Fails: On Eliminating Evaluation Apprehension from Attitude Measurement. *Journal of Personality and Social Psychology*, 1(1), 28–42.

Rosenthal, R (1991) *Meta-Analytic Procedures for Social Research*. London: Sage.

Rosenthal, R (1966) *Experimenter Effects in Behavioural Research*. New York: Appleton-Century-Crofts.

Rosenthal, R and Rosnow, RL (eds) (1969) *Artifact in Behavioural Research*. New York: Academic Press.

Rubia, K, Smith, A and Taylor, E (2007) Performance of Children with Attention Deficit Hyperactivity Disorder (ADHD) on a Test Battery of Impulsiveness. *Child Neuropsychology*, 13(3), 276–304.

Schafer, DR (2009) *Social and Personality Development*. 6th edition. California: Wadsworth Publishing.

Schaie, KW (1994) The Course of Adult Intellectual Development. *American Psychologist,* 49(4), 304–313.

Stevens, SS (1946) On the Theory of Scales of Measurement. *Science*, 103(2684), 677–680.

Tabachnick, BG and Fidell, LS (2001) *Using Multivariate Statistics*. 4th edition. Boston: Allyn & Bacon.

Tashakkori, A and Teddlie, C (eds) (2003) *Handbook of Mixed Methods in Social and Behavioral Research*. Thousand Oaks, CA: Sage.

Thurstone, LL (1929) Theory of Attitude Measurement. *Psychological Bulletin,* 36(3), 222–241.

Tileagă, C (2005) Accounting for Extreme Prejudice and Legitimating Blame in Talk About the Romanies. *Discourse and Society,* 16(5), 603–624.

van Beest, I and Williams, KD (2006) When Inclusion Costs and Ostracism Pays, Ostracism Still Hurts. *Journal of Personality and Social Psychology*, 91(5), 918–928.

Velleman, PF and Wilkinson, L (1993) Nominal, Ordinal, Interval, and Ratio Typologies Are Misleading. *The American Statistician*, 47(1), 65–72.

Wetherell, M (2001) Locating and Conducting Discourse Analytic Research, in Wetherell, M, Taylor, S and Yates, SJ (eds) *Discourse as Data: A Guide for Analysis*. London: Sage.

Williams, KD (2007) Ostracism. *Annual Review of Psychology*, 58(1), 425–452.

Wooffitt, R (2005) *Conversation Analysis and Discourse Analysis: A Comparative and Critical Introduction*. London: Sage.

Woolf, LM (1998) *Theoretical Perspectives Relevant to Developmental Psychology*. Available online at www.webster.edu/~woolflm/perspectives.html [Last accessed 4 April 2011]

Index